WRITERS AND THEIR

ISOBEL ARMSTRONG
General Editor

BRYAN LOUGHREY
Advisory Editor

CW00949795

English Translators
of Homer

ALEXANDER POPE
Pope in 1716, fingering the Iliad: *portrait by Sir Godfrey Kneller*

ENGLISH TRANSLATORS OF HOMER
from George Chapman to Christopher Logue

SIMEON UNDERWOOD

Northcote House
in association with the
British Council

Cover picture: Chapman, Homer and the Gods: the frontispiece to Chapman's translation of the lesser Homeric Poems (not now thought to be by Homer); copy of an 1858 facsimile of an original from 1624 or 1625.

© Copyright 1998 by Simeon Underwood

First published in 1998 by Northcote House Publishers Ltd, Plymbridge House, Estover Road, Plymouth PL6 7PY, United Kingdom.
Tel: +44 (01752) 202368 Fax: +44 (01752) 202330.

British Library Cataloguing-in-Publication Data
A catalogue record for this book is available from the British Library

ISBN 0-7463-0870-1

Typeset by PDQ Typesetting, Newcastle-under-Lyme
Printed and bound in the United Kingdom

This book is dedicted to my wife, Barbie,
with love and with thanks for all her help,
support, and patience.

Contents

Acknowledgements   viii

Note on the text   x

1   Translation: Some Issues   1   ✓

2   Translating Homer: Some Issues   8   ✓

3   George Chapman's Translation: An Elizabethan   16
    Homer?

4   Alexander Pope's Translation: An Augustan Homer?   29

5   E. V. Rieu's Translation: A Modern Homer?   43   ✓

6   Christopher Logue's Translation: A Modernist   56   ✓
    Homer?

Notes   69

Select bibliography   75

Index   80

Acknowledgements

I should like to thank the following: Bernard Gredley and Professor Michael Silk of King's College, London, for their encouragement of my interest in this area; Bryan Loughrey for his enthusiastic interest in my tentative proposals for this book; Professor Jacques Berthoud for general kindness and in particular help with sources of material on Chapman; Nicholas Lee of Bristol University Library for help with material from the Penguin archive on E. V. Rieu; Anne Rickards for help with passages translated from the French; the staff at Lancaster City Library for their prompt efficiency in handling requests for inter-library loans; and Brian Hulme for his guidance on technical matters.

The author and publishers are grateful to: Routledge & Kegan Paul for permission to quote part of the poem 'Sour Land' from *The Collected Poems of Sidney Keyes* (London, 1945); Martin Brian & O'Keeffe for permission to quote the poem 'On Looking into E. V. Rieu's Homer' from *Patrick Kavanagh: Collected Poems* (London, 1972); Penguin Books for permission to quote an extract from the essay 'Politics and the English Language' in George Orwell, *'Inside the Whale' and Other Essays* (Harmondsworth, 1962); Penguin Books for permission to quote extracts from the Introduction to and text of *The Odyssey*, trans. E. V. Rieu (Harmondsworth, 1946); Penguin Books for permission to quote an extract from the Introduction to *Virgil: The Pastoral Poems*, trans. E. V. Rieu (Harmondsworth, 1949); the University of Chicago Press for permission to quote extracts from the Foreword to and text of *The Iliad*, trans. Richmond Lattimore (Chicago, Ill. 1951); Robert Fitzgerald for permission to quote an extract from his translation of *The Iliad* (Oxford, 1984); Robert Fagles for permission to quote an extract from his translation of *The Iliad* (Harmondsworth, 1990); Christopher Logue and Faber & Faber for permission to quote extracts from the Introduction to and text of *War Music* (London, 1981) and from 'From Book XXI of Homer's *Iliad*', the latter as printed in Logue's *Selected Poems* (London, 1996); and Walter Shewring for permission to quote an extract from the Epilogue on translation appended to his translation of *The Odyssey* (Oxford, 1980).

Note on the Text

In view of the intended audience for this book, I have taken the liberty of modernizing some of the potentially distracting features of the older texts I have quoted. Thus, for example, in the quotations from George Chapman's translations of Homer, I have altered spellings and simplified punctuation; and in the quotations from Alexander Pope's translations, I have removed the capital letters which were characteristic of the period but are not now accepted usage.

Similarly and in the same spirit, in two passages quoted from A. T. Murray's Loeb translation of the *Iliad* (1924–5), there have been minor changes to vocabulary and word order.

1

Translation: Some Issues

In a little-known, deeply allegorical poem *'Euthymiae Raptus*, or The Tears of Peace' (1609), the poet George Chapman describes an encounter with the ghost of Homer. The scene calls to mind the long line of encounters between poets and their dead mentors, from Dante's meeting with Virgil in Canto 1 of *The Divine Comedy* to Eliot's with the 'familiar compound ghost' of 'Little Gidding'. The ghost identifies itself to Chapman thus:

> 'I am,' said he, 'that spirit Elysian
> That, in thy native air and on the hill
> Next Hitchin's left hand, did thy bosom fill
> With such a flood of soul that thou wert fain
> With acclamations of her rapture then
> To vent it to the echoes of the vale,
> When, meditating of me, a sweet gale
> Brought me upon thee; and thou didst inherit
> My true sense, for the time then, in my spirit;
> And I invisibly went prompting thee
> To those fair greens where thou didst english me.'
> Scarce he had uttered this, when well I knew
> It was my prince's Homer...
>
> (ll. 75–87)

This obscure passage describes what is in fact an important moment in English literature, for what Chapman meant by the phrase 'thou dids't english me' goes far beyond the act of translating the *Iliad* and the *Odyssey* from Greek into English. Elsewhere, in a poem 'To the Reader' with which he prefaces his translation of the *Iliad*, Chapman enjoins the reader to 'love' Homer 'as born in England: see him over-shine | All other-country poets...' (ll. 198–9). What is happening in these passages is that he is appropriating the Greek poet Homer into the English literary canon.

Why is this important to us now? 'Of all books extant in all kinds, Homer is the first and best,' Chapman wrote in yet another preface to the *Iliad*. And, as if in confirmation of this judgement, he has been 'english'd' since Chapman by many translators in successive generations, up to and including our own. Those Englishings are the subject of this book.

Within the limits of works in translation, Homer was by no means 'the first'. As we shall see in Chapter 3, the first translations of his works came upon the scene relatively late in the Renaissance period. Nor was he always regarded as 'the best'. Ovid and Virgil in turn had a much greater influence, at least until the start of the nineteenth century. However, this has now changed: most of the more than 200 translations of his works which have been attempted date from the twentieth century. Many bookshops have a large number of versions of Homer on their shelves, by different translators, some in verse and some in prose. Versions of Virgil and Ovid tend to be fewer in number; and other great works of world literature seem to be the preserve of a more limited number of translators – for example, versions of Dostoevsky and Proust in English are still largely the work of two translators each.

The main purpose of this book is to give an account of the reception of Homer into English literature, from Chapman onwards, mainly but not exclusively through the medium of the translations of different periods. Its strategy will be chronological but not comprehensive, in that I will focus on a key work for four different periods: the translations by Chapman, Pope, Rieu, and Logue. I will seek to place each of these in the context of its period, as translations can tell us much about wider literary attitudes and values; and they will also serve to illustrate something of the constantly changing attitudes to Homer and to the act of translation itself.

II

In the quarter century since J. M. Cohen wrote *English Translators and Translations* for this series (1962), translation studies has undergone a change in status, to the point where it is now recognized by many as a fully-fledged academic discipline.

Much of the academic activity of this period has been devoted to the psycholinguistic question of what actually happens during the act of translation, broken down variously into attempts to understand the nature of meaning itself and to show how meaning travels across the differences between one language and another. However, these areas are technical and outside the scope of this study.[1]

Another line of exploration, which is central to the purpose and argument of this book, concerns the relative priority to be given to the work being translated (what is sometimes called the source text) in relation to the work of translation (the target text). To put it another way: to what extent should a translator seek to be accurate and faithful to the original? Are accuracy and faithfulness necessarily the same thing? To what extent are accuracy and faithfulness even theoretically possible? What are the parameters of translation – should some works be regarded as paraphrases or free imitations rather than as translations proper?

The possible answers to these questions can be represented as a spectrum; and the position Vladimir Nabokov took up can be seen as one end of it:

> The person who desires to turn a literary masterpiece into another language has only one duty to perform, and this is to reproduce with absolute exactitude the whole text, and nothing but the text. . . . I take literalism to mean 'absolute accuracy'. If such accuracy sometimes results in the strange allegoric scene suggested by the phrase 'the letter has killed the spirit', only one reason can be imagined: there must have been something wrong with the original letter or with the original spirit, and this is not really a translator's concern.

Faced with the obvious problems to which this position gives rise, such as what to do when there are culture-specific allusions in the source text (Russian patronymic names, for example) or when there is no direct equivalent in the target language for the vocabulary or grammatical structure used in the source text, Nabokov had an ingenious solution: 'I want translations with copious footnotes, footnotes reaching up like skyscrapers to the top of this or that page so as to leave only the gleam of one textual line between commentary and eternity.'[2]

At the other end of the spectrum, and equally polemical in the way he presented his arguments, was Ezra Pound. He believed that a poem is more than its language, that it has underlying energies which go beyond the language in which it is written; and he used translation as a test bed for these ideas. He advised one translator, 'I'd like to see a "rewrite" as if you don't know the *words* of the original and were telling what happened'; and he wrote to another, 'Don't bother about the WORDS, translate the MEANING' (emphasis in original). This line of thought was also tied in to his method of 'luminous detail' (which was especially influential in shaping the agenda and the work of the Imagist movement).[3] He himself put his own theories into practice in a series of translations from a wide variety of languages, including the translation of a short extract from the *Odyssey* with which he began his own epic *The Cantos*. His translations are remarkable equally for their looseness in relation to their originals (some of which was arguably deliberate), the hostility they have attracted from scholars, and their power.

Between the positions taken by these two great figures of twentieth-century literature, a number of compromises and prescriptions are possible: that the approach to translation should be relative to the purpose for which it is intended – that, for example, translation for the stage has to be looser than translation for the page; or that the approach to translation should be relative to the audience for whom it is intended; or that translation can be allowed certain freedoms as long as it observes certain responsibilities, such as a responsibility to 'textual organicity' or 'an inventory of competences'.[4] Another variant is that the translator's responsibility can change in relation to the number of other available translations: the translator of a lesser-known original such as Apollonius Rhodius, it is argued, has to be faithful to the source text, whereas the translator of Homer at least has a choice.

What is common to all these compromise positions is that they are based on a clear order of priority between source and target text. The text being translated comes first, not just in time but in importance. Any translation is inevitably secondary and inferior. As the critic I. A. Richards wrote: 'The translator has first to reconcile himself to conceiving his art in terms of minimal loss and then to balance and adjudicate, as best he can, the claims of

4

the rival functions. His question is: Which sorts of loss will we take in order not to lose what?'[5]

Part of the significance of Pound's translations and ideas is that they offer a literary context in which the target text can be at least an equal of the source text. The significance of the most important recent writing about translation is that it goes further by dissolving these old arguments. In *After Babel*, a major study of the theory and processes of translation first published in 1975, George Steiner writes of 'the sterile triadic model' which underpins much writing and thinking on the subject: 'The perennial distinction between literalism, paraphrase and free imitation turns out to be wholly contingent. It has no precision or philosophic basis'.[6] In its place he proposes what he calls a 'hermeneutic of trust', a two-way process of exchange of energies between the source and target texts. Strict word-for-word literalism is unattainable and, moreover, involves denial of the translator's sensibility and the genius and historical development of his/her own language. A translation, however apparently 'close' it may be to its original, is not necessarily better or worse than the original: however, it is necessarily different, and Steiner would have us appreciate, in the double sense of recognize and relish, the differentness.

Moreover, on the more recent post-structural accounts, especially the work of Jacques Derrida, even the apparent fixity of source and target text is dissolved. Instead, they take their place within a continuum of production and reception, rather than standing at each end of it. The so-called source text is part of its own literary context and is a 'translation' of the works which have gone before it. The so-called target text may use other previous translations as source texts just as much as any putative 'original'; and each reading of the 'target text' is a further stage of translation in that it is individualized in the personal response of the person reading it (what is called 'reader-response theory'). These ideas are perhaps more complex even that Steiner's;[7] but, like Steiner, they encourage us to read translations in ways that liberate them – and us – from the priority of the source text.

III

Is it possible to choose between or even to reconcile these various viewpoints?

The liberatory arguments of Steiner and Derrida clearly have their merits. There is no possibility of neutrality in translation. It entails a continuous process of choice and commitment, going far beyond what is entailed in other, more single-dimensional forms of creative endeavour. Thus, those works of 'scholarly' translation which claim 'accuracy' or 'fidelity' or even 'objectivity' represent a position and an accompanying set of values every bit as much as those works which claim for themselves extreme artistic licence in the act of translation. Also, we need to be sensitive to the implications of the vocabulary we use in discussing translation and, above all, to get away from the polarities of inferiority/superiority and gain/loss. Instead, we should encourage ourselves to think of translations as works in their own right, rather than simply as reflections of an original.

But it is equally hard to deny that there is a human instinct to evaluate. In describing translations we almost inevitably find ourselves assessing the target text both against its source text and against the other available translations of the same work. When Steiner refers to the translations of Homer by Christopher Logue (discussed in Chapter 6 below) as 'licentious but numbingly powerful',[8] the phrase 'numbingly powerful' could function as evaluation of the work as poetry; but the adjective 'licentious' can function only as evaluation of the work as translation in relation to its source text. Similarly, when Peter Levi describes Robert Fagles's *Iliad* as 'an astonishing performance ... This should now become the standard translation for a new generation',[9] the word 'standard' implicitly conveys a judgement by benchmarking the translation ahead of other competing versions.

Such sweeping descriptions are tantalizingly attractive to the general reader, but without knowledge of the source language he/she is in no position to assess whether they are justified: which places a particular onus of critical responsibility on those who make them. Also, by the same arguments which would make the act of translation non-neutral, such acts of description and evaluation are non-neutral as well. This book seeks to offer an introduction not just to four major translations of Homer but also to ways of reading translations, by suggesting the kinds of information and the criteria we might look for and use in making such judgements for ourselves.

2

Translating Homer: Some Issues

I

Homer, source and subject of texts for translators, is also source
and subject of questions for scholars. The seventeenth-century
prose writer Sir Thomas Browne wrote in the *Urn Burial* (1658):
'What song the Syrens sang, or what name Achilles assumed
when he hid himself among women, though puzzling questions,
are not beyond all conjecture.' These were the questions
supposedly put by the Roman Emperor Tiberius to grammarians as examples of unanswerable questions at the limits of
scholarship. Browne tried to controvert the original point by
asserting that they are 'not beyond conjecture'; his purpose for
doing so is to draw a contrast between such questions and
the more immediate, mystical, and insoluble question of the
contents of the urns he was writing about – 'who were the
proprietaries of these bones, or what bodies these ashes made
up, were a question above antiquarism'. However, his assurance
about the Homeric questions would not be shared by the many
scholars who have written on Homer and his poems between
Browne's time and our own.

A first set of questions the scholars have addressed over this
period concerns Homer himself.

There is nothing to prove incontrovertibly that a historical
personage named Homer ever existed. His blindness, which is
an important motif for the approach of translators such as
Chapman, is a later tradition. We cannot even be sure of Homer
*him*self: the late-nineteenth-century writer Samuel Butler wrote
a book based on the premiss that the author of the *Odyssey* was
female, and there is nothing to disprove this apart from
overwhelming assumptions and stereotypes about authorship.

Nor do we know who wrote the poems down first or from where they derived the material they wrote down. It is clear that the poems are rooted in an oral tradition. A major piece of evidence for this is the stock formulae – godlike Achilles, rosy-fingered Dawn – which are one of their most immediate features. The existence of these formulae had been recognized from a very early stage; but our understanding of them has been deepened by the work of the American scholar Millman Parry and his followers in the first half of this century, who sought parallels in the epic recitations of oral bards in the Balkans and Eastern Europe. The effect of Parry's work was to characterize Homer as a 'culmination' of an oral tradition, which raises the question of the interface between oral poetry and literacy. The currently accepted view is that the alphabet was introduced into the Greek world around 800 BC and that the Homeric poems date from somewhere in the region of 750–700 BC: and one hypothesis extending out of Parry's work is that they 'are texts orally composed in performance, written down by dictation from that same performance'.[1] But this view is not universally shared. And, either way, not the least challenging question is how it has happened that the Western literary tradition should begin with two works of such massive length, assurance, and complexity.

Nor can we be sure that the *Iliad* and the *Odyssey* were 'written' by the same person. This question has been the subject of extensive scholarly debate since the end of the eighteenth century. The current majority view is for separate authors, with the *Odyssey* as the later work, its author steeped in the storyline and language of the *Iliad* but with his (her?) own values and interests.[2]

Although such questions pose enticing challenges for the Homeric scholar, they are also helpful to the literary commentator and translator in that they provide a liberation from the burden of biography. It is possible to address the works on their own terms, without having to acknowledge how they might also be a reflection of the values and interests of a historical personage complete with a personal history.

If the historicity of Homer gives rise to a first set of questions, a second set stems from the historicity of the events he is describing. For all the romance of the excavations of Schliemann in the north-east corner of Turkey at the end of the nineteenth century and the discovery of 'the jewels of Helen', there is again no incontrovertible evidence to prove an identification of the site at Hissarlik with the events Homer describes. There is no proof that Troy ever stood, let alone fell.

The uncertainty in this area is again an opportunity for literary commentators and translators, in that again it offers freedom from the need to take account of historical specificities. But it also provides a valuable metaphor for the modern relationship with Homer's text. Some scholars regard the text itself as an archaeological site, with an accumulation of textual and linguistic material, like debris, over an extended period.[3] This, however, is countered by the 'unitarian' approach, in which each of the works is seen (largely) as an artistically coherent whole.

II

With contextual and historical certainty and specificity stripped away, the translator is left addressing two poems.

On one level they are straightforward. The *Iliad* is a narrative describing events taking place towards the end of the ten-year siege of Troy by the Greeks, round a framework set by the doings of Achilles, the chief Greek warrior, who withdraws from the Greek army, in anger or some would say pique, and then returns to kill off Hector, his Trojan counterpart, thus clearing the way for the eventual Greek victory. The *Odyssey* describes the journey home by one of the Greek heroes, Odysseus, to his home country after the end of the Trojan War and his reintegration into a household which has been beset by suitors for his wife in his absence.

This apparent simplicity has coloured many critical attitudes and readings. In what is one of the most important pieces of Homeric criticism in the twentieth century, Eric Auerbach undertook a comparison in his book *Mimesis* between part of book 19 of the *Odyssey* and the sacrifice of Isaac in the Bible (Gen. 22:1 ff.), which led him to the conclusion that Homer's narrative technique was based on 'foregrounding': 'a continuous rhythmic procession of phenomena passes by, and never is there a form left fragmentary or half-illuminated, never a lacuna,

10

never a gap, never a glimpse of unplumbed depths'.[4] But this conception has now been largely rejected in favour of more sophisticated narratological analyses: the *Iliad* describes the events of forty days in the ten years of the Trojan War, with the action of the wider whole covered allusively in flashback or prophecy; while the various themes of identity in the *Odyssey*, such as naming and anonymity, concealment and non-recognition, lying and revelation, have proved fertile ground for postmodernist analysis. Retardation and suspense are a vital element of the technique of both poems, not least in the very passage of the *Odyssey* on which Auerbach bases his analysis.

III

There are several issues largely specific to Homer, as distinct from other source texts, which have posed dilemmas for the translator: and I want to pick out four of them as potential tests for identifying the various approaches different translators take to the Homeric original.

The first is in the content of the works. The storylines of both poems are given an extra dimension through the divine machinery of gods and goddesses which features prominently throughout. Many of their actions are capricious and seem to lie outside what we would recognize as a consistent ethical and moral code; their involvement in the affairs of the human heroes raises questions of determinism and free will. It is clear that this troubled early thinkers: in one of the earliest works of literary criticism, ascribed to Longinus and tentatively dated to the first century AD, there is the paradox 'Homer seems to have done everything in his power to makes gods of the men fighting at Troy, and men of the gods'.[5] If this was problematic to the classical world, it has been an even greater concern to translators working at later stages of the Western Christian tradition.

The second issue is also in the content of the works, and mirrors the first. According to the early Greek philosopher Xenophanes Homer 'attributed to the Gods all the things | which among men are shameful and blameworthy – | theft and adultery and mutual deception':[6] and the men of the *Iliad* and the *Odyssey* were not slow to learn from the Gods' example. Achilles has a major argument with the commander of the Greek troops in the first book of the *Iliad*, spends the next eighteen books sulking and taking no part in the action, and then in the next four books commits a number of acts of brutal cruelty. Odysseus tells a sequence of increasingly elaborate lies in the second half of the *Odyssey*, through which he deceives his household and even his wife about his true identity. These are not good role models for writers and translators seeking to promote ideas about heroism and chivalry. The poems do not offer clear-cut moral or ethical messages such as wrong being righted, or good winning through against the odds.

Moreover, both works are very much men's poems. One feminist critic has written:

> The true female condition in Homer was this: total exclusion from political power and participation in public life; subordination to the head of the family and submission to his punishment; and finally, ideological segregation. Forbidden to think about anything but domestic matters, the woman cannot even talk about male matters. Faithless, weak, fickle, she was regarded with suspicion.[7]

This is not an imbalance which has as yet troubled any of the translators of Homer: but the growth of scholarship on women and women's issues in the life and literature of the classical world may mean that it cannot be ignored in the future.

The third issue is the language of the works. Homer's language is a composite drawn from several different regional dialects with their variants, often for the same word or grammatical form; in some ways it can be regarded as a literary pastiche, not dissimilar to the language used by Spenser in *The Faerie Queene* or by Chatterton in his historical poems. It is also clearly a medium for oral poetry; and one of the main features which identifies it as such is Homer's extensive use of repeated oral formulae. These come in various forms, such as the use of epithets for individual characters – 'swift-footed Achilles' 'horse-taming Hector'. There is no particular consistency to their use – different heroes are described with the same epithet, the same hero is described with different epithets. Nor is there any clear logic – ships are described as swift-keeled even when they are being put up in harbour. A major consideration seems to be metrical variation. Another form is the extended passage over several lines to describe, for example, daybreak, ritual sacrifice, and feasting. These present a problem for translators: if Homer uses identical text in two different places, should the translator seek to replicate it, at risk of puzzling or, worse still, boring a modern reader?

The fourth and final issue combines content and language. Put simply, what are the main characteristics of the Homeric style which the translator should seek to convey? In a highly influential formulation Matthew Arnold, the nineteenth-century critic and scholar, wrote as follows:

> ... the translator of Homer should above all be penetrated by a sense of four qualities of his author: – that he is eminently rapid; that he is eminently plain and direct, both in the evolution of his thought and in the expression of it, that is, both in his syntax and in his words; that he is eminently plain and direct in the substance of his thought, that is, in his matter and ideas; and, finally, that he is eminently noble.[8]

More recently, Michael Silk, a classical scholar, has reformulated Arnold in terms of the alternative concepts of immediacy and stylization: Homer, Silk argues, is 'immediate' in his idiom; yet he is also highly stylized, in the sense of being highly conventionalized and often schematic. Silk's concept of immediacy brings together the features Arnold discusses under 'rapidity', 'plainness', and 'directness'; it includes concrete vocabulary, a tendency to frankness, through which the grand and heroic are sometimes presented in relation to everyday objects or events. Stylization is his addition to Arnold, and covers features such as the stereotyping of scenes such as combat or the use of epithets and extended epic simile.[9] Silk also shows how the two actively interrelate: the example he chooses is the passage in book 22 of the *Iliad* where Achilles chases Hector round the walls of Troy and past 'broad washing-tanks, fine and made of stone, where the wives and fair daughters of the Trojans used to wash their bright clothing in the time of peace' (more of this passage is given below). Neoclassical requirements of decorum or Arnold's notion of nobility are inappropriate here: the heroic and the everyday coexist.

An area where the need to balance immediacy and stylization becomes a particularly important issue for translators is in the representation of direct speech. 'About half of the total extent of the *Iliad* and the *Odyssey* consists of direct speech of the participants. Seldom in either are there more than fifty continuous lines of uninterrupted narrative.'[10] The *Odyssey* in particular contains a sequence of four books where the narrative is told in the form of a first-person speech by Odysseus himself. Yet there is very little attempt to differentiate between different speech patterns, even between gods, heroes and servants. Ezra Pound wrote that Homer's quality of 'the authentic cadence of speech; the absolute conviction that the words used, let us say by Achilles to the "dog-faced", chicken-hearted Agamemnon, are in the actual swing of words spoken' had not been captured by any of his translators.[11] And this has become an even greater challenge for translators now that it is the norm rather than the exception for writers, whether in verse or prose, to seek to reproduce 'natural' speech patterns.

IV

What, then, is the overall effect of Homer against which translations are to be measured? In a book about translation this is not a question which is going to be answered easily or without self-consciousness. The following fuller version of the passage from book 22 of the *Iliad* referred to above aims to be literal in the sense of providing a one-for-one equivalent of the words in the Greek text in an order which is close to that of the original:

> So Hector pondered as he waited, and Achilles came near to him, the equal of Enyalius the god of war, warrior of the flashing helmet; he was brandishing over his right shoulder the Pelian ash, his terrible spear, and all around the bronze flashed like the gleam of blazing fire or of the sun as it rises. But trembling took hold of Hector when he became aware of him, and he did not dare to wait any longer where he was, but left the gates behind him and fled in fear; and Achilles son of Peleus rushed after him, trusting in his speed of foot. In the same way that a falcon in the mountains, swiftest of winged things, swoops lightly after a trembling dove: the dove flees before it, and hard of heart it continually darts at the dove with shrill cries, and its heart tells it to seize the dove: that was the way in which Achilles in his fury sped straight on, and Hector fled beneath the wall of the Trojans, and moved his limbs swiftly. They sped past the

watch-tower and the wind-blown wild fig-tree, continually moving away from under the wall along the wagon-track; and they came to the fair-flowing fountains where the two springs which feed eddying Scamander well up. One of them flows with warm water, and round about it smoke goes up as from a blazing fire; while even in summer the other flows forth as cold as hail or chill snow or the ice that water forms. And there near these very springs are broad washing-tanks, fine and made of stone, where the wives and fair daughters of the Trojans used to wash their bright clothing in the time of peace before the sons of the Achaeans came. By this place they ran, one fleeing, and one pursuing. In front a good man fled, but a much greater man pursued him swiftly: for it was not for a sacrificial animal or a bull's hide, the kinds of prizes men win in footraces, that they were striving: but it was for the life of horse-taming Hector that they ran. And it was like when single-hoofed horses that are winners of prizes move swiftly round the turning-points, and some great prize is set out, perhaps a tripod or a woman, in honour of a warrior who is dead; even so these two circled three times with swift feet around the city of Priam; and all the gods gazed upon them.   (*Il*. 22, 131–65).[12]

But this is only one voice. What makes Homer such a rich source both for translation and for translation analysis is the length of the works and their longevity. The former allows scope for a variety of readings; the latter means that the text has accumulated a very wide variety of scholarly and literary approaches to itself. The result is that, in line with the postmodernist principles discussed in the previous chapter, the translator is forced to make choices.

The richness of Homer is such that he even provides his own metaphor for this variety. In the first line of the first book of the *Odyssey* Homer uses the Greek world *polutropos* as an adjective to describe Odysseus. In various translations this is rendered as 'the man of many devices', 'that man so ready at need', 'for shrewdness famed and genius versatile', 'the man of many ways', 'the man for wisdom's various arts renowned', 'that resourceful man', 'one who was never at a loss', 'the various-minded man', or 'the man of wide-ranging spirit'.[13] The wide range is indicative of Homer's own polytropism, which we shall explore further through our four translations.

3

George Chapman's Translation: An Elizabethan Homer?

I

John Keats first encountered Chapman's translation of Homer in October 1816 at the age of 20 through his friend Charles Cowden Clarke:

> One scene I could not fail to introduce to him – the shipwreck of Ulysses, in the fifth book of the *Odysseis*, and I had the reward of one of his delighted stares upon reading the following lines:
>
>> Then forth he came, his both knees falt'ring, both
>> His strong hands hanging down, and all with froth
>> His cheeks and nostrils flowing, voice and breath
>> Spent to all use, and down he sank to death.
>> The sea had soak'd his heart through...

According to Cowden Clarke's account, Keats stayed with him until dawn and by ten o'clock the same morning sent round to him a poem: which is the famous sonnet 'On First Looking into Chapman's Homer':

> Much have I travelled in the realms of gold,
>   And many goodly states and kingdoms seen;
>   Round many western islands have I been
> Which bards in fealty to Apollo hold.
> Oft of one wide expanse had I been told
>   That deep-browed Homer ruled as his demesne;
>   Yet did I never breathe its pure serene
> Till I heard Chapman speak out loud and bold:
> Then felt I like some watcher of the skies
>   When a new planet swims into his ken;
> Or like stout Cortez when with eagle eyes
>   He stared at the Pacific – and all his men

> Looked at each other with a wild surmise –
> Silent, upon a peak in Darien.

However, for all the lavish praise Keats bestowed on the translation on first encountering it, there is nothing in his letters and papers to suggest an unusually close or sustained engagement with either Homer or Chapman. The correspondence for August 1820 even shows that he had to buy a copy of Chapman's works for a friend to replace one which he had borrowed and then lost (worse still, the lost copy may have been a 1616 First Edition).

Moreover, in its turn Keats's poem has often been misunderstood. An article by one of the leading contemporary translators of Homer says of early versions of Homer that 'we used to think... that a poem built a perfect world – that Homer stood behind us, always offering what Keats had called the "realms of gold"'.[1] This is at best misleading, at worst wrong: within the symbolic geography of Keats's sonnet, the 'realms of gold' are other poetry and possibly other translations of Homer: but the best of what Homer has to offer, as revealed by Chapman's translation, is represented by the newly discovered Pacific Ocean, and this is reached only by crossing the 'realms of gold' and leaving them behind.

But the final irony is the worst. Although Keats's sonnet has become one of the most famous set pieces of English literature, Chapman's Homer, its subject, is at the time of writing out of print in the United Kingdom. All that is available to the contemporary reader are a few short extracts in anthologies.

II

The Elizabethan period in which Chapman was writing is often regarded as a 'Golden Age' of English translation. There was, for example, a succession of translations of Virgil's *Aeneid*; and Ovid was another writer to receive particularly extensive coverage. Nor was attention confined to classical literature: there were also several important translations from near-contemporary literature in romance languages.

What, however, is conspicuous by its absence from any list of this kind is translation from the Greek. The translation of

Plutarch by North from which Shakespeare took both plot lines and text may seem to be an exception to this: but North translated it via a French intermediary. Although the works of Plato were very important as an influence on Elizabethan thought, they came at second hand through the Italian translations of Ficino, which had first appeared in 1484. Although the tragedies of the Latin playwright Seneca were freely available and legitimized the more gruesome excesses of the Elizabethan and Jacobean theatres, the plays of the Greek tragedians Aeschylus, Sophocles, and Euripides, which are central to our appreciation of Greek culture and thought, were translated only rarely before the second half of the eighteenth century. The only major act of translation from the Greek prior to Chapman was through the great Elizabethan translations of the Bible, culminating in the Authorized Version of 1611.

Nevertheless, the name of Homer and the subject matter of the Trojan War was familiar to readers long before Homer's text was available to them. It had been transmitted at second hand, through the prose chronicles of Dictys and Dares, popularly conceived to be eyewitness accounts of the Trojan War from the Greek and Trojan viewpoints respectively (but probably written in the third and fifth centuries AD). It is their works, mediated through various sources and in particular through the Italian poet Boccaccio, which provide the source material for Chaucer's *Troilus and Criseyde* (finished about 1385), not Homer's *Iliad* – Troilus is in fact mentioned once in the *Iliad* and Cressida not at all. Another important route of transmission of the Trojan story into the English literary tradition is Lydgate's *The Troy Book* (written between 1412 and 1420), an account of the various legends surrounding the Trojan War which runs to over 30,000 lines in length. Chaucer and Lydgate in their turn seem to have been the primary sources for Shakespeare's *Troilus and Cressida* (written in 1601 or 1602).

The first English Homer was a translation of the first ten books of the *Iliad* by Arthur Hall, published in 1581. Hall was a landed gentleman and briefly a Member of Parliament before being barred from the House after a series of misdemeanours which included making 'sundry lewd speeches' inside and outside the House, serious affray, criticism of the Speaker, over-argumentativeness, and debt. His motivation for undertaking the task seems to have been to please his patrons, the Cecil family, as protection in a life which was notorious for troubles with the law; and it is possible that some of the translation was undertaken while he was in prison.

His translation was carried out at second hand from the Greek text, via an intermediary French version by Hugues Salel which had been published in 1555. Salel's version is notable for its short five-beat verse line and its extensive use of polysyllabic rhyme words. Perhaps as a result of working from this source, the characterizing features of Homer which we discussed in the previous chapter are not evident in Hall's version.[2] Also, it was completed before or independently of the Elizabethan reception of Renaissance influences, with the result that there is little sign of interest in or experimentation with language. Instead, as Hall's biographer comments, 'many lines suggest the mono-tonous jog-trot of a Middle English epic rather than the great body of verse which inevitably presents itself to our minds on hearing the word "Elizabethan" '.[3]

Hall used a longer line and simpler language than Salel. But his version tends towards bathos and doggerel, and makes much use of verbal padding. Here is his version of one of the most famous 'purple passages' of the *Iliad*:

And often shall the passers-by say, Look who yonder is,
The wife of valiant Hector lo! who in the field with his
Such fame and great renown did get, when Grecians compassed round
The great and mighty town of Troy and tore it to the ground.
How great to hear my name rehearsed shall then thy dolours be
And that my help thou canst not have eft to recover thee.
But ere the wailings I will hear of thee my captive wife,
The earth shall hap this corpse of mine, and I will lose my life.'
With this the valiant prince doth hide his cark and inward grief,
And out doth put his hands to take his son, the pretty leaf,
A little pretty bulchion fat, seeing the dreadful crest
And armour, cries and calls his nurse, and nuzzles in her breast.
With this the courteous parents they smile at the pretty grace
Of that the babe, and Hector he his son for to embrace
Doth set aside his lofty helm, he him doth coll and cuss,
With pleasant mind he holds him soft and formed his prayers thus...

(*Il.* 6, 460–75)

III

Unlike Hall, Chapman had access to a Greek text, in the form of the edition by Jean de Sponde (Spondanus) which had been published in Basle in 1583. But facing the Greek text in Spondanus' version was a parallel Latin translation by Andreas Divus, which in fact seems to have formed the basis for Chapman's translation. In addition Chapman also used a wide range of secondary sources, such as lexicons, commentaries, and versions of the original in Latin, Italian, or French. Even his Greek dictionary, Scapula's lexicon of 1580, was Greek to Latin rather than Greek to English. His translation of Homer was a collation of these various sources, rather than an engagement with Homer's Greek text. There is no reason to suppose that Chapman was translating directly from the Greek: like Hall, he was working largely at second hand. Nor should this surprise us: although Latin was an established feature of the curriculum at the grammar schools or universities in the sixteenth century, this was not the case with Greek.

In spite of this, Chapman regarded himself as having a special affinity with Homer, to an extent one critic terms self-aggrandizement. The evidence is abundant in the various prefatory poems and forewords Chapman provided. His translations carried with them their own commentaries, covering Homer's text, Chapman's own translation, and the secondary sources he was using. He used them to make a connected set of claims, in part about language and in part about the ideas behind the text (the latter derived from Plato and Neoplatonism via Ficino), to show that he alone had discerned Homer's true meaning and had done so through poetry:

> Poetry for Chapman becomes almost equivalent to innate knowledge, which by divine inspiration is awakened within, being the well-spring of mankind's buried divinity. Poetry, then, is at once the end and means of man's natural desire for the divine. Chapman does occasionally talk about poetry in the normal way as referring to the process for making poems. Often, however, he means by poetry the whole emergence of sequences associated with divine disclosure and the human potential to be carried along this stream...[4]

This conception of poetry is particularly linked to Homer through

20

the motif of Homer's blindness, which becomes a symbol of special insight. It also led Chapman to abuse time and again the very scholars on whom he was reliant for his understanding of Homer's text, on the grounds that they do not understand what they are dealing with: 'I dissent from all other translators and interpreters that ever assayed exposition of this miraculous poem, especially where the divine rapture is most exempt from capacity in grammarians merely and grammatical critics, and where the inward sense or soul of the sacred muse is only within eye-shot of a poetical spirit's inspection...'.[5]

These various threads come together in a passage from the introductory poem 'To the Reader' where he is commenting on his use of 'needful periphrases' by 'great learned men':

> But, as the illustration of the Sun
>   Should be attempted by the erring stars,
> They failed to search his deep and treasurous heart.
>   The cause was since they wanted the fit key
> Of Nature, in their down-right strength of Art,
>   With poesy to open poesy –
> Which in my poem of the mysteries
>   Revealed in Homer I will prove...

(ll. 137–44)

IV

Chapman produced his *Iliad* in irregular tranches over an extended period. In 1598 *Seven Books of the Iliades of Homer, Prince of Poets* (books 1, 2, and 7 to 11 inclusive) was published; also, later in the year, a separate publication, *Achilles Shield*, an extract from book 18 of the *Iliad*.[6] In 1609 an edition of the first twelve books was published, with the first two heavily revised, the others from the first 1598 volume left unaltered, and the remaining books added. This was followed two years later by a full and complete text, *The Iliads of Homer, Prince of Poets, Never Before in any Language Truly Translated*. Chapman tells his readers in a preface that 'less than fifteen weeks was the time in which all the last twelve books were entirely new translated': if this is true, such momentum is a particularly remarkable achievement considering the technical difficulties he faced; it may also be a further illustration of his near-mystic relationship with Homer.

The commentaries on the later material contain responses to critical comment on the earlier versions, most notably where he rails at 'a certain envious windfucker' (possibly Ben Jonson) 'that hovers up and down...buzzing into every ear my detraction, affirming that I turn Homer out of the Latin only, etc. – that sets all his associates and the whole rabble of my maligners on their wings with him to...poison my reputation'.

His *Odysseys of Homer, Translated According to the Greek* was published between 1614 and 1616. It is in many ways a very different work, not least in that Chapman used a different metre: where the versions of the *Iliad* are written in rhyming couplets in a metre called 'fourteeners' (as in the extract from Hall above), for the *Odyssey* the couplets are in a ten-syllable metre which was rare for the period but became much more common later. There is no obvious explanation for the change.

In the development between the various versions of the *Iliad* it is possible to trace an underlying pattern of changing purposes. Like that of Hall, the translation was initially undertaken for a particular patron; but unlike that of Hall, its purpose may have been not merely to please the patron but also to provide coded messages. Chapman's translation has at least two overlapping levels of overlay on top of the text itself: the allegorical and the hermetic. Poetry for Chapman, as we have seen earlier, existed both to hide the meaning of ancient texts from the general reader and to reveal it only to initiates.

The *Iliad* is on the face of it unpromising material for allegory of any kind: as we saw in the last chapter, the heroes, especially Achilles, carry out a number of unheroic, or at the least unchivalrous, actions. But in his early versions Chapman seems to have modified the text in order to draw parallels between Achilles and the Elizabethan warrior/hero Essex. The versions of 1598 were dedicated to Essex as the 'most true Achilles, whom by sacred prophecy Homer did but prefigure in his admirable object and in whose unmatched virtues shine the dignities of the soul and the whole excellence of royal humanity'. The difficult relations between Achilles and the leaders of the Greek army, which caused the former to retreat from the War, may be seen as mirrored in those between Essex and Elizabeth. Also, the apparently random decision to translate *Achilles Shield* in 1598 may be explained by the historical fact that Essex was making preparations for a military expedition to Ireland at the time.

However, the expedition proved ill-fated and Essex an unfortunate patron to have backed: and evidence for this is provided in the various significant changes Chapman made between the 1598 and 1609 versions. Chapman reconceptualized Achilles by emphasizing and condemning the excesses he commits in the later books, notably in dragging the dead body of Hector round the walls of Troy; and he modified the more overt political interpolations of the earlier versions. The transition is very visible: one critic claims to see him shift from attention to the hero to attention to the artist; another from a chivalric mode to a psychological mode.[7]

If Chapman's allegory in the *Iliad* is political, in the *Odyssey* it is moral. In a footnote to line 1 of book 1 Chapman uses a Latin definition for the word *polutropos* I mentioned at the end of Chapter 1, which translates as 'a man whose spirit' (*ingenium*) 'as if through many and varied routes is turned' (*vertitur*: which could also mean transformed, even translated) 'into truth'. Another footnote, occasioned by an elaboration on two words in the Greek, remarks on 'the allegory driven through the whole *Odysseys*': 'Deciphering the intangling of the wisest in his affections and the torments that breed in every pious mind; to be thereby hindered to arrive, so directly as he desires, at the proper and only true natural country of every worthy man, whose haven is heaven and the next life, to which this life is but a sea in continual aesture and vexation.'

In part on the basis of these footnotes, one critic has argued that Chapman drew out of Homer a 'dynamic allegory' which was 'evolutionary and complex instead of static and schematic':

> Chapman did what no extant scholar, critic, writer of commentaries, allegorical interpreter or translator contemporary, medieval or ancient, had ever done. He reconciled what many of them held to be Homer's moral idealism with instances of Odysseus' immoral behaviour which they had ignored, suppressed or distorted to fit their preconceptions about the poem....[He] saw Ulysses as an emergent, dynamic character, one beset by passions that constantly threatened to destroy him, but struggling through repeated failures towards an ideal which he very gradually discovered in the process.[8]

As part of this allegory, a moral contrast is set up between

Odysseus himself and his fellow-sailors, who as weaker mortals are beset by passions which destroy them.

There is much room for argument over this analysis, on two grounds. First, it is not clear that this allegory was in Homer in the first place. Also, this account tends to exclude much of what happens in the second half of the poem, when Odysseus has returned in disguise to his own palace. In particular, Penelope has little place in these moral patterns. Secondly, it gives great emphasis to a small number of relatively short passages in a very long poem. Nevertheless, there can be little doubt that Chapman saw himself as having a responsibility to draw out his author's moral messages as part of his special relationship with Homer.

Here then is an illustration of an important development in the approach to translation: between Hall and Chapman has entered the concept that translation may in itself have a purpose beyond the mere transmission of the original text.

V

Chapman is neither faithful to Homer nor an easy read, even when allowances are made for the state of Greek learning at the time, the sources he was using, his stance on the hermetic nature of poetry, and the wider purposes he was seeking to achieve.

One area of difficulty is that his translation of the Greek Homer is full of Latinisms, many – but not all – of which can be traced directly either to the Latin translations or to the Greek: Latin lexicon he was using as his support. In any extended passage of either poem the reader is likely to come across a striking usage involving a Latinate polysyllable, and in some of these cases Chapman clearly intends that an understanding of the etymology will help to a deeper understanding of the meaning.

The same historicity may also go some way towards explaining another immediately visible feature of Chapman's Homer, notably its structural complexity within the long sentences. This is very much at odds with the characteristic simplicity of Homer's own style: if Homer uses a long sentence (and, given the oral basis of Homer, it is a moot point what a sentence actually is), it normally comprises a series of short sentences held together by simple conjunctions; the more complex structures of later classical Greek with their dependent clauses and genitive absolutes are infrequent.

There are several other technical devices Chapman uses frequently which serve to reinforce his complexity, notably compound word forms he invents sometimes to compress vocabulary – 'care-and-lineament-resolving sleep', 'wise-in-chaste-wit-worthy-wife' – and sometimes to represent the Homeric formulae – 'Atreus' tame-horse son', 'the helm-graced Hector'. Another frequent device is ellipsis, often in order to generate momentum.

The other major stylistic divergence between Chapman and his original lies in his insertion of small-scale, routine metaphor into the Greek text – perhaps much of what he adds could be viewed as an Elizabethan translator's range of ornamentation and cliché.

At its best, the apparent difficulty turns into intellectual rigour and profundity of a kind which goes beyond anything less strong-willed translations can achieve. At its worst, the effect is clotted and jumbled. Often the gap between the two is very small. Here is his version of the passage from book 22 of the *Iliad* which I used in the previous chapter:

These thoughts employed his stay: and now Achilles comes; now near
His Mars-like presence terribly came brandishing his spear.
His right arm shook it: his bright arms like day came glittering on,
Like fire-light or the light of Heaven shot from the rising Sun.
This sight outwrought discourse. Cold fear shook Hector from his
    stand.
No more stay now; all ports were left; he fled in fear the hand
Of that fear-master, who hawk-like, air's swiftest passenger,
That holds a timorous dove in chase, and with command doth bear
His fiery onset – the dove hastes – the hawk comes whizzing on –
This way and that he turns and winds and cuffs the pigeon,
And till he truss it his great spirit lays hot charge on his wing:
So urged Achilles Hector's flight; so still fear's point did sting
His troubled spirit. His knees wrought hard; along the wall he flew
In that fair chariot way that runs beneath the tower of view
And Troy's wild fig-tree, till they reached where those two mother-
    springs
Of deep Scamander poured abroad their silver murmurings –
One warm and casts out fumes as fire, the other cold as snow

Or hail dissolved. And when the sun made ardent summer glow,
There water's concrete crystal shined, near which were cisterns made
All paved and clear, where Trojan wives and their fair daughters had
Laundry for their fine linen weeds, in times of cleanly peace
Before the Grecians brought their siege. These captains noted these,
One flying, th'other in pursuit: a strong man flew before,
A stronger followed him by far, and close up to him bore.
Both did their best, for neither now ran for a sacrifice,
Or for the sacrificer's hide (our runners' usual prize).
These ran for tame-horse Hector's soul. And as two running steeds,
Backed in some set race for a game that tries their swiftest speeds
(A tripod or a woman given for some man's funerals),
Such speed made these men, and on foot ran thrice about the walls.
  The Gods beheld them, all much moved...

(*Il.* 22, 115–44)

VI

Despite the efforts of the 'envious windfucker', the early
reception of Chapman's Homer seems to have been highly
favourable. A poem by Samuel Sheppard published in 1651, less
than twenty years after Chapman's death, began as follows:

> What none before durst ever venture on
> Unto our wonder is by Chapman done,
> Who by his skill hath made Great Homer's song
> To vail its bonnet to our English tongue,
> So that the learned well may question it
> Whether in Greek or English Homer writ?[9]

However, perhaps predictably, it fell out of whatever favour it
may have had during the eighteenth century. Samuel Johnson
in his *Life of Pope* (1781) called it 'now totally neglected', but
added that it 'seems to have been popular almost to the end of
the last century'.[10]

Written only thirty-five years after Johnson's comments, Keats's
sonnet was the high water mark of appreciation of Chapman's
Homer. But it is by no means the only example of Romantic
fervour in support of his version. In 1808, six years earlier,
Coleridge sent a copy of the translation to Sara Hutchinson with
an accompanying letter in which he said that Chapman's version
of the *Odyssey* 'has no look, no air, of a translation. It is as truly an

original poem as the *Fairy Queen* [*sic*]':

> Chapman writes & feels as a Poet – as Homer might have written had he lived in England in the reign of Queen Elizabeth – in short, it is an exquisite poem, in spite of its frequent & perverse quaintnesses & harshnesses, which are however amply repaid by almost unexampled sweetness & beauty of language, all over spirit & feeling. In the main it is an English Heroic Poem, the *tale* of which is borrowed from the Greek – ... (spelling and emphasis as original)[11]

But the tide of favour turned quickly. Matthew Arnold had respect for Chapman's poetic merits but was troubled by what he termed his 'curious complexity' of thought. His judgement was that 'Homer expresses himself like a man of adult reason, Chapman like a man whose reason has not yet cleared itself'.[12]

Others of his generation were shorter on respect. In a book on Chapman's works published in 1875 the poet Swinburne wrote: 'For all his labours in the field of Greek translation, no poet was ever less of a Greek in style or spirit. He enters the serene temples and handles the holy vessels of Hellenic art with the stride and grasp of a high-handed and a high-minded barbarian' – itself as telling about Swinburne and his notions of Hellenism as it is about Chapman.[13]

An image of Chapman as an obscurantist, bitter pedant, based in the identification of him with the character of Holofernes in Shakespeare's *Love's Labour's Lost*, began to emerge in the nineteenth century. It was taken up and developed by T. S. Eliot, who relocated him with the Metaphysical Poets rather than in the Elizabethan intellectual environment: 'in Chapman...there is a direct sensuous apprehension of thought, or a recreation of thought into feeling, which is exactly what we find in Donne.'[14]

The low water mark was perhaps reached in an earlier volume in this series, *George Chapman*, by the distinguished Elizabethan scholar M. C. Bradbrook (1977), who wrote:

> as Destiny and Choice, he found a rôle in the ennobling of the language by translation as a form of public service; the Authorized Version of the Bible was being prepared as he laboured at Homer, whom he probably thought of as second only to Holy Writ. Alas for the result; as Dr Johnson said of women's preaching, it is not well done, but you are surprised to find it done at all.

But even the apparently objective and disinterested judgements of scholars need to be contextualized; and a recent work on Chapman, under the revealing title *The Mystification of George Chapman*,[15] goes some way both towards explaining why some of Chapman's critics, notably Dryden, Swinburne, and Eliot, said what they said when they said it, and towards denying the stereotyping of Chapman's poetry as obscure. The same exercise of rehabilitation now needs to be done for his translations of Homer by making them more widely available.

4

Alexander Pope's Translation: An Augustan Homer?

I

The poem 'Sour Land' by the Second World War poet Sidney Keyes, who was killed in battle at the age of 20, has an explanatory note affixed to it: 'At Stanton Harcourt in Oxfordshire there is an ancient tower in which Pope completed the fifth book of his *Iliad*, when illness and disillusionment were beginning to oppress him.' This text is filled out mainly in the second of the three parts of the poem:

> So to his perch appropriate with owls
> The old lame poet would repair,
> When sorrow like a tapeworm in his bowels
> Drove him to Troy and other men's despair.
>
> His lame leg twisted on the spiral stair,
> He cursed the harsher canker in his heart;
> Then in the turret he would scrawl and glare
> And long to pull his enemies apart.
>
> When night came knocking at the panes
> And bats' thin screeching pierced his head,
> He thought of copulation in the lanes
> And bit his nails and praised the glorious dead.
>
> At dawn the lapwings cried and he awoke
> From dreams of Paris drowned in Helen's hair;
> He drew his pride about him like a cloak
> To face again the agony of the stair.

A memorable picture indeed, the ageing poet fighting what Keyes elsewhere in the poem calls 'the running demon, thought' in a 'landscape of bulbous elm and stubble'. The only problem is that in virtually every respect the picture is an imaginative fantasy.

For example, the translations of Homer were not the work of Pope's old age: quite the contrary. One of the most important keys to understanding them is that they were done when he was relatively young. Although he was already a well-established poet, the first part of his *Iliad* was published in June 1715 when he was only 27 and the final part of his *Odyssey* in 1726, some eighteen years before his death at the early age of 56. They were a calculated attempt on Pope's part both to secure his financial position and to confirm his reputation with his contemporaries; and they succeeded in both aims.[1]

As an extension of this, and in complete contrast to Keyes's depiction of an intensely misanthropic Pope working in isolation and driven by disillusionment and despair, Pope's translations of Homer were intimately related to the polite London society, both literary and otherwise, of their time. Although he spent some time at Stanton Harcourt in the later stages of writing the *Iliad*, it was an affected and very sociable 'retreat' from fashionable circles in the city. The works were funded and published by subscription, involving the highest in the land in their production. Pope could afford to make assumptions about his audience's knowledge of both Homer and the English literary tradition; and, particularly in their use and appreciation of the visual arts, these translations of the oldest extant works in Western literature reflected all that was most modern in artistic connoiseurship.

II

Between Chapman and Pope the standing of Homer, in literary, moral, and cultural terms, had undergone two major challenges.

The first challenge had come from Virgil's *Aeneid*. A hierarchy of poetic endeavour had been formed in neoclassical literary theorizing, and epic was the apex. But with the prioritizing of epic came accompanying notions, later codified into conventions, of what an epic should be, in terms of moral purpose and stylistic decorum: to which the *Aeneid* conformed more closely than either of Homer's poems.

Between 1650 and 1710 five complete versions of the *Aeneid* had appeared, as well as at least seventeen versions of parts of it; most of the incomplete versions were translations of book 4, the story of the doomed love between Dido and Aeneas for which there is no parallel in Homer. The most important complete version for Pope's purposes was the one by John Dryden, which was first published in 1697. By contrast, between Chapman and Pope there had been only two complete translations of Homer, by John Ogilby (*Iliad* (1660), *Odyssey* (1665)) and by Thomas Hobbes, now better known as a philosopher and author of *Leviathan* (*Odyssey* (1675), *Iliad* (1676)), as well as a handful of translations of short passages and single books from the two poems, notably versions by Dryden and Congreve. Virgil was more readily available, and central to the literary consciousness, including through the continuing influence of Milton's 'Lycidas' (1637) and *Paradise Lost* (first printed in 1667).

Part of the comparison was based in morality. In contrast to Homer's unheroic heroes, Virgil's Aeneas is an almost flawless paragon of self-control driven by duty, to the point where modern counter-criticism finds itself having to excuse him from the charge of being something of a prig. More generally, some of the features of Homer's style, such as the repetitions and the use of similes drawn from everyday life, were regarded as inappropriate to epic decorum: where Virgil, though in many ways working closely from Homer, was seen as having lived in a more refined civilization and as having ironed out such flaws.

The second challenge was on a broader scale. The English attitude to Homer in the seventeenth century had been coloured by a debate in French intellectual circles which was styled the Quarrel between the Ancients and the Moderns.[2] This had a considerable impact in English literary circles, as the main works were all translated and available in a short space of time through what one critic has called 'the cosmopolitan nature of neo-classical culture'.[3] The subject of the Quarrel was the argument of the Moderns about the imperfections, indeed irrelevance, of classical models in relation to the perfections of contemporary French society. A key work was the *Parallèle des Anciens et des Modernes* by Charles Perrault, published in four volumes between 1688 and 1697, whose theme is summed up in the argument of an earlier poem entitled 'Le Siècle de Louis le

Grand': 'It seemed to me ... sheer ingratitude not to want to open our eyes to the beauties of our century, on which Heaven has bestowed so much knowledge which it previously denied to the whole of Antiquity.' Literature is only one of the many fields of human culture and endeavour over which Perrault's text ranges; but within it Homer is his main target. He criticizes his poems as the product of a primitive age, and characterizes them as an assemblage of shorter poems by a variety of different authors.

Thus, bringing the two arguments together, Perrault wrote that Homer's works seemed to him to be 'full of grossness, childishness and extravagance', where the corresponding virtues of Virgil were 'elegance, gravity and reason'. The cause of this difference is merely chronological: 'it comes about simply as a result of the difference between the times when they wrote, and from the fact that Virgil is more modern than Homer by eight or nine hundred years.'

Subsequently the focus of the Quarrel moved from general cultural issues to the specific issue of the standing of Homer's works, and between 1711 and 1716 Anne Dacier and Antoine de la Motte produced translations and pamphlets in support of and against Homer respectively.

Although Anne Dacier's translation and arguments were to be of significant use and importance to him, Pope went to some lengths to steer a path between the positions of both the Ancients and the Moderns. In an account of the aims of the translator in his Preface to the *Iliad*, he comments that

> ... with whatever judgement and study a man may proceed or with whatever happiness he may perform such a work, he must hope to please but a few, those only who have at once a taste of poetry and competent learning. For to satisfy such as want either is not in the nature of this undertaking; since a mere modern wit can like nothing that is not modern, and a pedant nothing that is not Greek.[4]

Thus the decision to translate Homer ran against the contemporary fashion. Even if his route to translating Virgil had been cut off by Dryden, his motive for translating Homer seems to have a positive desire to reaffirm the qualities and the standing of the *Iliad* and the *Odyssey*.

This is the context in which we should read one of the most frequently quoted lines in translation criticism. Richard Bentley, one of the greatest classical scholars of the time, is famously reputed to have said 'It is a pretty poem, Mr Pope, but you must not call it Homer'. What this is normally taken to mean is that Pope's Homer is an artefact of the cultural values of its own time but not a true reflection of Homer. But what it may also mean is that Pope's Homer does not reflect Bentley's Homer. Bentley's own reading of Homer, which in many particulars follows that of Perrault, was highly reductive:

> Take my word for it, poor Homer, in those circumstances and early times, had never such aspiring thoughts. He wrote a sequel of songs and rhapsodies, to be sung by himself for small earnings and good cheer, at festivals and other days of merriment; the *Ilias* he made for the men, and the *Odysseis* for the other sex. These loose songs were not collected together in the form of an Epic Poem, till Pisistratus' time about 500 years later.[5]

The paradox is that, although many modern critics make much of Bentley's dictum, Pope's Homer, with its assertion of the poetic unity, coherence, and quality of the original, is much closer to our modern readings of Homer than Bentley's own.

III

Pope chose to produce his Homer on the basis of subscription from its potential purchasers. This device was, as Johnson points out in his *Life of Pope* (1781), not wholly unusual for the day. At the time he launched the subscription scheme, Pope was already well known for earlier works such as 'Essay on Criticism', 'The Rape of the Lock', and 'Windsor Forest'. However, Johnson also provides some interesting context on the terms of the subscription:

> [Pope] offered an English *Iliad* to subscribers, in six volumes in quarto, for six guineas; a sum, according to the value of money at that time, by no means inconsiderable, and greater than I believe to have been ever asked before. His proposal, however, was very favourably received; and the patrons of literature were busy to recommend his undertaking and promote his interest.[6]

The subscription lists themselves are a very revealing account of Pope's audience. Over 30 per cent of the subscribers for the *Iliad* belong to the peerage, and over 40 per cent are titled. The list for the *Odyssey* is headed 'The King/The Prince/The Princess'.[7] Their absence from the earlier list may have been reluctance on their part to give support to a young Roman Catholic author in the year of the first Jacobite Uprising. Their presence on the later list is evidence of how successful Pope had been in his ambition of using the Homer translations to establish his reputation.

We know a great deal about the production process for the *Iliad* and the *Odyssey* from various sources, including the extensive correspondence which has survived. The early stages of the *Iliad* were approached with optimism, if apprehension:

> 'Tis no comfortable prospect to be reflecting, that so long a siege as that of Troy lies upon my hands, and the campagne above half over, before I have made any progress. Indeed the Greek fortification upon a nearer approach does not appear so formidable as it did, and I am almost apt to flatter my self, that Homer secretly seems inclined to a correspondence with me, in letting me into a good part of his intentions. [30 January 1713–14][8]

In the second sentence there are overtones of Chapman's claims to a special and secret relationship with Homer; and elsewhere in the correspondence there are verbal motifs of intense withdrawal and possession which also recall Chapman.

This early hopefulness, however, gave way to anxiety, mainly at the size of the task he had set himself; and his friend Joseph Spence recorded the following comments in his *Anecdotes* (first published posthumously in 1820):

> The *Iliad* took me up six years; and during that time, and particularly the first part of it, I was often under great pain and apprehensions. Though I conquered the thoughts of it in the day, they would frighten me in the night. I dreamed often of being engaged in a long journey and that I should never get to the end of it. This made so strong an impression upon me that I sometimes dream of it still: of being engaged in that translation; and got about half way through it: and being embarrassed and under dreads of never completing it.[9]

The word 'embarrassed' is particularly significant in reinforcing the social context of the translations.

Accordingly, when he came to produce the *Odyssey*, he arranged to share the labour with two colleagues, William Broome and Elijah Fenton; they produced first drafts of twelve

34

of the twenty-four books, which Pope 'revised', although there was much controversy even at the time about the actual extent of the revision. Pope himself said of it that it was 'an exacter version than that of the *Iliad* where all the drudgery was my own'.[10] Pope's *Odyssey* was held in lower esteem than his *Iliad* both by his contemporaries and subsequently: and for this reason, for the remainder of this chapter I shall draw my examples from the latter.

The correspondence also shows Pope signing off from translation after the completion of the *Odyssey*: on 23 November 1725 he wrote 'When I translate again I will be hanged; nay I will do something to deserve to be hanged, which is worse, rather than drudge for such a world as is no judge of your labour. I'll sooner write something to anger it, than to please it.'[11]

For his translation Pope seems to have used some of the same apparatus of commentary and criticism as Chapman, including the edition of the text by Spondanus, together with material which had come into print subsequently, notably a new edition of Homer published in 1711 and the French prose translation published in the same year by Anne Dacier.

There is some question about the quality of Pope's own Greek, not least because he was largely self-taught, a fact which gave rise to scepticism on the part of some eighteenth-century scholars. Clearly his Greek was better than Chapman's. Equally clearly he was aware that it had its limits; and his efforts were supported by a coterie of scholars to whom he had easy access. This was an area in which he was sensitive to the point of being defensive, not least because the translations and the intellectual debate of the previous century had given the literary circles who were subscribing to his edition a clear sense both of Homer and of what they expected of a translation. Also, the general level of Greek learning at the major schools and universities was, simply, more advanced than in Chapman's time.

This may also account for Pope's decision from the outset to accompany the translation by an extensive commentary. Johnson's view of this aspect of the work is somewhat cynical: 'Notes were likewise to be provided; for the six volumes would have been very little more than six pamphlets without them.'[12] However, this is to ignore the value of the commentary in underpinning the translation and in supporting the claims Pope was making about Homer. Some of it is given over to scholarly material, including comments on the life and customs of the civilizations described in the poems; this is the area where he seems to have derived much of the material from his friends, from Mme Dacier's pamphlets, and from an earlier commentary by the twelfth-century Byzantine scholiast Eustathius. Some of it takes the form of advanced criticism, poet to poet, on matters of technique and poetic effect: much of this material is highly perceptive, anticipating the lines later criticism would take; and much of it is couched in superlatives, such as 'Nothing is more fine than this...' (3. 487), 'It is impossible for anything to be better imagined than these two speeches' (21. 84), 'A man must have no taste for poetry that does not admire this sublime description' (24. 417), and numerous other examples. These superlatives need to be read as an assertion of Homer's primacy against the countervailing evaluation of Virgil.

However, this admiration is on occasion offset by doubt:

> I sometimes think that I am in respect to Homer much like Sancho Panza with regard to Don Quixote. I believe upon the whole that no mortal ever came near him for wisdom, learning, and all good qualities. But sometimes there are certain starts which I cannot tell what to make of, and am forced to own that my master is a little out of the way, if not quite beside himself. (*Il*. 16. 1032)

It is also in the commentary that Pope's invocations of the visual arts and the notion of connoiseurship come into their own – the roll-call of artists mentioned in the notes includes Raphael, Rubens, Julio Romano, Guido, Spagnoletto, and Salvator Rosa; the notes include sentiments such as 'poetry (at least in Homer) is truly a speaking picture' (*Il*. 21. 41). A separate and very full analysis of the Shield of Achilles (book 18) ends with a testimonial by the painter Sir Godfrey Kneller to Homer's powers as an artist and Pope's as a connoisseur.

But perhaps the most interesting aspect is his use of the commentary to reinforce the standing of Homer in relation to the epic tradition. There are frequent quotations from earlier translations, notably that of Chapman. Allusions to the epic tradition through Virgil, Milton, and Dryden abound. The Bible is frequently invoked: in the Preface to his *Iliad*, Pope wrote:

36

> This pure and noble simplicity is nowhere in such perfection as in the Scripture and our author [i.e. Homer]. One may affirm with all respect to the inspired writings that the Divine Spirit made use of no other words but what were intelligible and common to men at that time and in that part of the world; and as Homer is the author nearest to those, his Style must of course bear a greater resemblance to the sacred Books than that of any other writer.[13]

Sometimes the purpose of his allusiveness is specific and local, as, for example, when Pope invokes *Paradise Lost* and the Garden of Eden with a view to excusing by association what would otherwise be seen as the low vulgarity of book 14 of the *Iliad*, in which the goddess Juno seduces her husband Zeus in order to distract his attention from what is going on in the battle outside Troy. More generally, the purpose is to assert Pope's own view of Homer as a conscious and coherent artist who is all-important because of his position at the head of the epic tradition and at the same time to assert Pope's own scholarship and consequently his eligibility as translator.

Where Chapman had written his notes in hostile opposition to predecessors and contemporaries alike, Pope writes his as a synthesizing encyclopaedia on ways of reading his translation.

IV

Pope's Homer, both the *Iliad* and the *Odyssey*, is in the heroic couplet, a rhymed form which was predominant for most serious poetry at the time. It is striking that, for all the space afforded to him by the length of the originals he is translating, Pope makes only occasional use of textual variety through enjambment, either within or beyond the couplet – in this respect his approach to poetic form is very different from Chapman's. This is partly a function of the stage in Pope's career at which the translations were written: closed couplets and internal balance are more characteristic of his earlier works. The rhyme words themselves are mostly monosyllabic. Also conspicuous by their absence are the sharp wit and word play devices familiar from works such as 'The Rape of the Lock': although here it may be that he is constrained by working from a source text. Nevertheless, he has available to him a repertoire of devices such as balance, chiasmus, and onomatopoeia to ensure that the couplet form does not become monotonous.

His diction is set in part by prevailing conventions. The repertoire of effects open to the epic poet had been spelt out by writers such as Joseph Addison: in one of his Spectator essays on Milton's *Paradise Lost* (*Spectator* 285 (January 1712)), Addison, borrowing from Aristotle, cited three stylistic devices as requisite to the sublimity of a heroic poem: the use of metaphors; the use of idioms of other languages, under which he includes modification of the word orders of prose by devices such as 'the placing the adjective after the substantive, the transposition of words, the turning the adjective into a substantive'; and 'the lengthening of a phrase by the addition of words, which may either be inserted or omitted, as also by the extending or contracting of particular words by the insertion or omission of certain syllables'. All of these are evident in Pope's translations.

Other immediately noticeable features are an extensive use of abstract personification; the use of Roman rather than Greek names for the Gods; and an avoidance of Homer's low-life imagery. This is consistent with contemporary attitudes to the level of elevation of language and thought appropriate to the epic genre. But his squeamishness does not extend to Homer's descriptions of the bloody excesses of warfare:

> So the fierce coursers, as the chariot rolls,
> Tread down whole ranks, and crush out heroes' souls.
> Dashed from their hoofs while o'er the dead they fly,
> Black, bloody drops the smoking chariot dye:
> The spikey wheels through heaps of carnage tore;
> And thick the groaning axles dropped with gore.

> (*Il.* 20. 581–6)[14]

A further defining characteristic is Pope's attempt to render the Homeric original as a series of pictures or tableaux. Action is stopped and the details are carefully arranged in a painterly manner; and, in case the reader misses this, Pope often draws attention to it in the Commentary so that text and notes work together to achieve the overall effect.

Here, then, is Pope's rendition of the same passage used in the two previous chapters:

Thus pond'ring, like a God the Greek drew nigh;
His dreadful plumage nodded from on high;
The Pelian jav'lin, in his better hand,
Shot trembling rays that glittered o'er the land;
And on his breast the beamy splendors shone
Like Jove's own lightning or the rising sun.
As Hector sees, unusual terrors rise,
Struck by some God, he fears, recedes, and flies.
He leaves the gates, he leaves the walls behind.
Achilles follows like the winged wind.
Thus at the panting dove a falcon flies,
(The swiftest racer of the liquid skies)
Just when he holds or thinks he holds his prey,
Obliquely wheeling through th'aerial way;
With open beak and shrilling cries he springs,
And aims his claws, and shoots upon his wings:
No less fore-right the rapid chase they held,
One urged by fury, one by fear impelled;
Now circling round the walls their course maintain,
Where the high watch-tow'r overlooks the plain;
Now where the fig-trees spread their umbrage broad,
(A wider compass) smoke along the road.
Next by Scamander's double source they bound,
Where two famed fountains burst the parted ground;
This hot through scorching clefts is seen to rise,
With exhalations steaming to the skies;
That the green banks in summer's heat o'erflows,
Like crystal clear, and cold as winter-snows.
Each gushing fount a marble cistern fills,
Whose polished bed receives the falling rills;
Where Trojan dames (e'er yet alarmed by Greece)
Washed their fair garments in the days of peace.
By these they passed, one chasing, one in flight,
(The mighty fled, pursued by stronger might)
Swift was the course; no vulgar prize they play,
No vulgar victim must reward the day,
(Such as in races crown the speedy strife),
The prize contended was great Hector's life.
As when some hero's fun'rals are decreed
In grateful honour of the mighty dead;
Where high rewards the vig'rous youth inflame,
(Some golden tripod, or some lovely dame),
The panting coursers swiftly turn the goal,
And with them turns the raised spectator's soul.

> Thus three times round the Trojan wall they fly;
> The gazing Gods lean forward from the sky...

> (*Il.* 22. 173–218)

Pope uses forty-six lines compared to Chapman's thirty-one (although the lines are shorter). Only six of the rhyme words are not monosyllables; only five of the couplets are not closed, and of these two come within one of the epic similes. Also, there are several choice examples of epic diction – e.g. 'the liquid skies' and 'th'aerial way'.

If we are disappointed that Pope chose not to counter the contemporary conventions and expectations by affirming his own individuality, there are several counter-arguments. First, we need to keep in mind the purpose of Pope's Homer within his *œuvre*, as an attempt to confirm his growing reputation with the literary and social establishment of the day. Secondly, we need to imagine reading Pope as if we have read Dryden and Milton beforehand: although his debt to them on occasion extends to direct quotation, there are marked differences, and Pope's translatorial style often has a lighter tone to it. Thirdly and more generally, we need to avoid imposing anachronistic notions about the role of originality in the poetic imagination. The stereotype of the 'Augustan Age' is set by the phrase itself, with its Latinate origins; and another phrase used to caricature the period is 'The Age of Reason' ('reason' was one of the virtues Perrault attributed to Virgil in the phrase in Chapter 4, Section II). But contemporary literary criticism is now tending to reread the eighteenth century away from this stereotype. A recent book on Pope's *Iliad* is subtitled 'Homer in the Age of Passion'.[15] Pope's approach to the *Iliad* can be reinterpreted along similar lines. For example, his choice to translate Homer was, as we have seen, not necessarily consistent with 'Augustan' values. Moreover, the Preface makes it clear that he saw Homer as a poet of 'Fire' and 'invention', which are presented as opposites to reason and self-restraint – in another characteristic superlative from the Preface, Pope remarked: 'It is to the strength of this amazing invention we are to attribute that unequalled fire and rapture which is so forcible in Homer, that no man of a true poetical spirit is master of himself while he reads him. What he writes is of the most animated nature imaginable; everything moves, everything lives, and is put in action.'[16]

V

In its day and its own terms, Pope's Homer was one of the wonders of its age. Although he had cavilled at Pope's epic diction in one of his early essays,[17] in the *Life of Pope*, written more than twenty years later, Johnson called the translation 'a performance which no age or nation can pretend to equal' and famously said of it, 'It is certainly the noblest version of poetry which the world has ever seen; and its publication must therefore be considered as one of the great events in the annals of learning.' He gave over a large proportion of the biographical section of the *Life* to an account of the writing and production of the translations and rather less to Pope's 'original' works. In the evaluative section his tone is adulatory:

> He cultivated our language with so much diligence and art that he has left in his Homer a treasure of poetical elegances to posterity. His version may be said to have tuned the English tongue; for since its appearance no writer, however deficient in other powers, has wanted melody. Such a series of lines, so elaborately corrected and so sweetly modulated, took possession of the public ear; the vulgar was enamoured of the poem, and the learned wondered at the translation.[18]

But the wheel turned remarkably quickly. In 1785, only four years after Johnson's *Life of Pope* was published, the poet Cowper wrote of Pope's translations:

> The *Iliad* and the *Odyssey*, in his hands, have no more of the air of antiquity than if he had himself invented them. Their simplicity is overwhelmed with a profusion of fine things, which, however they may strike the eye at first sight, make no amends for the greater beauties which they conceal.... He is often turgid, often tame, often careless, and, to what cause it was owing I will not even surmise, upon many occasions has given an interpretation of whole passages utterly beside their meaning.[19]

His distrust of Pope's accuracy in conveying both text and style of Homer's original caused him to produce his own translations of both the *Iliad* and the *Odyssey*, which appeared in 1791.

In the *Biographia Literaria* Coleridge describes Pope's *Iliad* as 'that astonishing product of matchless talent and ingenuity': but the equivocation of these terms is amplified later in a footnote in chapter 2 of the same work: 'In the course of my lectures, I had occasion to point out the almost faultless position and choice of words in Mr Pope's *original* compositions, particularly in his satires and moral essays, for the purpose of comparing them with his translations of Homer which I do not stand alone in regarding as the main source of our pseudo-poetic diction' (emphasis in original); and in 1831 Robert Southey wrote to his friend Caroline Bowles 'Pope's Homer has done more than...all other books towards the corruption of our poetry'.[20]

The violence of this reaction matches and vindicates the claims Johnson made for the central significance of Pope's Homer. Also, it becomes possible to see the praise given by Coleridge and Keats to Chapman's translation, as outlined in the last chapter, as an equal and opposite reaction to their view of Pope's translation.

Arnold's comments on Pope's translation suggest that the anger of the reaction subsided but not its substance:

> Homer invariably composes 'with his eye on the object', whether the object be a moral or a material one: Pope composes with his eye on his style, into which he translates his object, whatever it is. That, therefore, which Homer conveys to us immediately, Pope conveys to us through a medium. He aims at turning Homer's sentiments pointedly and rhetorically; at investing Homer's description with ornament and dignity. A sentiment may be changed by being put into a pointed and oratorical form, yet may still be very effective in that form; but a description, the moment it takes its eyes off that which it is to describe, and begins to think of ornamenting itself, is worthless.[21]

The terms 'rhetoric', 'dignity', 'oratory', and 'ornament' show that by this time (1861) the stereotype of the Augustan age was firmly established. The complexity of the process I have tried to describe whereby Pope was working not only with but also against the prevailing tastes and conventions of his age had been flattened out.

5

E. V. Rieu's Translation: A Modern Homer?

I

Patrick Kavanagh's poem 'On Looking into E. V. Rieu's Homer' (1951) clearly borrows its title from Keats, but not much else:

> Like Achilles you had a goddess for mother,
> For only the half-god can see
> The immortal in things mortal;
> The far-frightened surprise in a crow's flight
> Or the moonlight
> That stays for ever in a tree.
>
> In stubble fields the ghosts of corn are
> The important spirits that imagination heeds.
> Nothing dies; there are no empty
> Spaces in the cleanest-reaped fields.
>
> It was no human weakness when you flung
> Your body prostrate on a cabbage drill –
> Heart-broken with Priam for Hector ravaged;
> You did not know why you cried,
> This was the night he died –
> Most wonderful-horrible
> October evening among those cabbages.
>
> The intensity that radiated from
> The Far Field Rock – you afterwards denied –
> Was the half-god seeing his half-brothers
> Joking on the fabulous mountain-side.

Where Chapman appears in Keats's poem both in person and implicitly in the person of Cortez, it is, as we shall see, characteristic that E. V. Rieu should be absent from a poem named after him. But his approach to Homer is nevertheless

43

very much a subject of Kavanagh's poem. On one level, like Kavanagh's better-known 'Epic', it describes a marvelling vision of the presence of Homer and Homeric heroes in rural Ireland. But on another level it is a meditation on the four-way relationship between the epic and the everyday, the poetic and prose. Where Rieu's Homer is a translation of epic poetry into everyday prose, Kavanagh is showing not only that the epic exists in the everyday but that the everyday does not have to be prose.

Kavanagh's is not a poetry that Pope, for example, would recognize. Where there is elevation of diction, it is almost immediately repudiated; the rhyme scheme is spontaneous and slips into and out of view; the vocabulary is indecorous. It is typical that the reader is left unsure whether 'ravaged' is really meant to rhyme with 'cabbages'. Nevertheless it is undoubtedly poetry, as, for example, defined by George Steiner:

> The distinctive beat of any given tongue, that sustaining under-current of inflexion, pitch relations, habits of stress, which give a particular motion to prose, is concentrated in poetry so that it acts as an overt, characteristic force.... a poem enlists the maximal range of linguistic means ... it articulates the code of any given language at its most incisive ... [1]

The juxtaposition of the Homers of E. V. Rieu and Patrick Kavanagh and the distinctions drawn by Steiner raise the set of issues which will dominate the remaining sections of this book. In what circumstances is it legitimate for a translator to carry the original work across the boundary from poetry to prose? To what extent is it possible to identify this boundary, any more than it is possible to identify the boundary between the human and the divine in Kavanagh's Irish countryside?

II

Historically there have been two main motives for crossing the boundary from Homer's poetry to a prose translation. The first, which is more negative, is the belief that the verse forms in the target language are inadequate as a vehicle for the Homeric source. The second, which is more positive, believes that the prose forms in the target language have their own capabilities and range of references which can be used to bring out aspects of the source's potential.

One of the earliest prose translations of Homer was produced by Anne Dacier in 1711, whom we encountered in the previous chapter as champion of the Ancients in the Quarrel between the Ancients and the Moderns and a source for some of Pope's thinking (and many of his notes). Her reasons for choosing prose stem from her reverence for Homer and are thus representative of the first of the lines of argument outlined above:

> A translator can say in prose everything Homer has said: this is something which he can never do in verse, above all in our language, where it is necessary to make changes, cuts and adjustments. So what Homer has thought and said, even if it has to be expressed more simply and less poetically than he actually said it, is certainly of more value than everything one is forced to attribute to him when translating him in verse.[2]

Her attitudes to verse and prose need to be set in the context of the priority given in seventeenth-century French and English to the heroic couplet as a verse form: more than many other verse forms, the couplet, as the examples from Pope show, imposes constraints of a kind which make changes, cuts, and adjustments necessary. But she is also saying that prose is not an ideal vehicle for translating Homer either, given its inability to convey his complexity and poetry. The point of using it is that it affords the lesser loss.

Arnold's lectures 'On Translating Homer' are in the same vein: although he stops short of advocating prose as a medium for translating the poet, his main subjects are both the actual shortcomings of existing translations, including Chapman and Pope (as in the quotations in Chapter 3, Section VI, and Chapter 4, Section V), and, as important, the theoretical shortcomings of most of the available poetic forms.

The second of the lines of argument outlined above came into being with the emergence of the novel. Many of those who translate Homer into prose do so because they see his poems, and the *Odyssey* in particular, as novels. Moreover, the compliment is returned: many of those who write novels lean heavily on the mythic and narrative templates set in the first works of European literature.

Just as early printing mimics the illuminated manuscripts it is soon to supersede, so the early novel is deeply concerned with its relation with the epic. This is particularly prominent in the works of Henry Fielding. *Tom Jones* (1749), for example, has a chapter (IV.8) entitled 'A battle sung by the Muse in the Homerican style, and which none but the classical reader can taste', which burlesques epic by using its conventions to describe the low-life fight between Molly Seagrim and the people of the village in the churchyard:

> Recount, O Muse, the names of those who fell on this fatal day. First, Jemmy Tweddle felt on his hinder head the direful bone. Him the pleasant banks of sweetly-winding Stour had nourished, where first he learnt the vocal art, with which, wandering up and down at wakes and fairs, he cheered the rural nymphs and swains, when upon the green they interweaved the sprightly dance; while he himself stood fiddling and jumping to his own music. How little now avails his fiddle! He thumps the verdant floor with his carcass.

In a later chapter (VII. 12) Tom Jones meets a character who mispronounces the name Homer as 'homo', which is also the Latin word for Man: a clear statement of Homer's central place in Fielding's universe.

Having been in at the beginning of the novel, Homer continues to have a place in many of the divergent forms it later takes on. It can be argued that the modernist novel begins only when Homer, 'a stripling, blind, with a tapping cane', and his characters walk the streets of Dublin in Joyce's *Ulysses*.

III

This understanding that the novel and Homeric epic are intimately related reappears as one of the main justifications for prose translation of the verse original. Moreover, although it would not be realistic to draw parallels between the development of the novel and of the prose translations, something of the diversity the novel takes on is reflected in some of the approaches taken by different prose translations.

It would, for example, be possible to see the nineteenth-century historical novel of Scott and Harrison Ainsworth reflected in the translations of the *Odyssey* by Lang and Butcher (1879) and the *Iliad* by Lang, Leaf, and Myers (1883). The introduction to the former explains why they are in prose:

The epics are, in a way, and as far as manners and institutions are concerned, historical documents. Whoever regards them in this way, must wish to read them exactly as they have reached us, without modern ornament, with nothing added or omitted. He must recognise, with Mr. Matthew Arnold, that what he now wants, namely, the simple truth about the matter of the poem, can only be given in prose, 'for in a verse translation no original work is any longer recognisable'.... We have tried to transfer, not all the truth about the poem, but the historical truth, into English.

In their pursuit of the historical truth and as a means of asserting historical authenticity, Lang and his collaborators deliberately chose to translate into 'a somewhat antiquated prose'. Their main model is the vocabulary and rhythms of the Authorized Version of the Bible, from which they borrow heavily on the grounds that 'the Greek epic dialect, like the English of our Bible, was a thing of slow growth and composite nature ... the Biblical English seems as nearly analogous to the Epic Greek, as anything that our tongue has to offer' (echoes here of Pope's comments on the linguistic relationship between Homer and the Scriptures in Chapter 4, Section III). Thus the passage at the start of book 11 of the *Odyssey* which Pound used in his *Cantos* reads as follows:

'Now when we had gone down to the ship and to the sea, first of all we drew the ship unto the fair salt sea, and placed the mast and sails in the black ship, and took those sheep and put them therein, and ourselves too climbed on board, sorrowing, and shedding big tears. And in the wake of our black-prowed ship Circe of the braided tresses, an awful goddess of mortal speech, sent a welcome breeze that filled the sails, a good companion. And we set in order all the gear throughout the ship and sat us down; and the wind and the helmsman guided our barque. And all day long her sails were stretched in her seafaring; and the sun sank and all the ways were darkened.'[3]

The prose used by the late Victorian writer and thinker Samuel Butler in his translations of the *Iliad* (1898) and the *Odyssey* (1900) is very different. In a jotting headed 'Translations from Verse into Prose' in his *Notebooks* (published posthumously in 1912), Butler comments:

Whenever this is attempted, great licence must be allowed to the translator in getting rid of all those poetical common forms which

47

are foreign to the genius of prose. If the work is to be translated into prose, let it be into such prose as we write and speak among ourselves. A volume of poetical prose, i.e. affected prose, had better be in verse outright at once.[4]

Elsewhere he describes the Lang versions as 'making a mummy'.

His own readings of Homer and his translation strategy were at odds both with the historicizing approach of the Lang translations and with the romanticizing approach of the Edwardian society which carried the Homeric values of comradeship and honour, personified in particular in the love between Achilles and Patroclus, with it into the trenches of the First World War. Butler was more concerned with the human beings in the poems. In 1897 he published a work entitled *The Authoress of the Odyssey*, in which he argued that the *Odyssey* was in fact written by a woman and that the woman who wrote it was the character Nausicaa who appears in the earlier books. He based his argument on clues drawn from the interior of the poem, features such as 'mistakes and self-betrayals' in technical descriptions of a kind a man would not make, or various traits summarized in one chapter heading as 'jealousy for the honour and dignity of women – severity against those who have disgraced their sex – love of small religious observances – of preaching – of white lies and small play-acting – of having things both ways – and of money'. Another strand of 'evidence' is the overall 'charm' of the work, especially in comparison to the *Iliad*. This belief is carried through to his translation of the *Odyssey*, which he overtly uses as a 'proof' of the argument.

Much of what Butler says about the genders may seem to us to be working from stereotypes: but at least he is prepared to countenance and explore this as a possibility. If there is an analogy with the novel here, it might be with the 'problem novels' of writers such as Meredith, which sought to explore the wider possibilities in human relations and reactions, in particular in terms of differences and similarities between the genders.

Another prose version is equally idiosyncratic. After returning from his own adventures in the Middle East, T. E. Lawrence, 'Lawrence of Arabia', translated the *Odyssey* under the pseudonym T. E. Shaw (published in 1932). For our purposes the most interesting part of it is Lawrence's 'Translator's Note', in which he describes the *Odyssey* as 'the oldest book worth reading for its story and the first novel of Europe'. Like Butler, he has a particular conception of what is entailed in translating into prose: 'Wherever choice offered between a poor and a rich word richness had it, to raise the colour.' Like Butler, also, he goes on to reconstruct Homer out of the evidence available in the poems, even if the result is rather different:

> In four years of living with this novel [sic] I have tried to deduce the author from his self-betrayal in the work. I found a book-worm, no longer young, living from home, a mainlander, city-bred and domestic. Married but not exclusively, a dog-lover, often hungry and thirsty, dark-haired....He loved the rural scene as only a citizen can. No farmer, he had learned the points of a good olive tree. He is all adrift when it comes to fighting, and had not seen deaths in battle. He had sailed upon and watched the sea with a palpitant concern, seafaring being not his trade. As a minor sportsman he had seen wild boars at bay and heard tall yarns of lions.

Much of this, of course, is given in order to show that Homer is everything Shaw/Lawrence is not. But, perhaps surprisingly, this translation is not an adventure story after the manner of John Buchan (whose own work carries a number of allusions to Homer). The Homeric original has served to constrain the potential offered by the analogy with the novel form or with the translator's own biography.

IV

In Shaw's Homer, Odysseus, Homer, and Lawrence of Arabia vie for the reader's attention. E. V. Rieu, by contrast, is concerned to maintain the anonymity of both translator and author, from the use of his initials onwards. Rieu signs off the Introduction to his *Odyssey* abruptly, saying 'I had better come to an end, rather than...fall into the most heinous crime that a translator can commit, which is to interpose the veil of his own personality between his original and the reader'.[5] And he succeeds in veiling his own personality almost completely. Unlike Butler and Shaw/Lawrence, there is no extensive apologia to explain his attitude either to Homer or to translation; unlike Chapman and Pope, there is no commentary from which we might draw clues for ourselves. As a result, both the translator and his translation have avoided any of the critical attention which has been given to the other major translations.

Paradoxically, this covert *Odyssey*, first published by Penguin in 1946, became a best-seller. Over 100,000 copies were published within a few months. After fifty years the figure for sales stands at over 3 million copies; and only one title in all of Penguin's lengthy lists, *Lady Chatterley's Lover*, has sold more copies. It has been reprinted a large number of times; a revised edition, produced by Rieu's son, was published in 1991; and a facsimile edition of the 1946 original was published in 1996 to mark the fiftieth anniversary of the Penguin Classics series. Rieu's *Iliad* followed in 1950; generally regarded at the time as a less successful translation, it has sold a mere 1.5 million copies.

The *Odyssey* was produced as the first of the Penguin Classics series, of which Rieu was the founding editor. The purpose, as stated on the endpapers of some of the earliest volumes in the series, was

> to provide English-speaking readers with new versions of the finest and most enduring of the foreign classics, ancient, medieval and modern. It was felt that many opportunities for enjoyment were denied to those unfamiliar with the languages concerned, by the stilted, old-fashioned and otherwise un-English style which has too often been adopted by translators.

Another publicity blurb for the series, dating from July 1946, is even more explicit, referring to 'the unnecessary difficulties and erudition, the archaic flavour and the foreign idiom that renders so many existing translations repellent to modern taste'. This suggests that the conscious archaizing of translations such as the Lang versions was one of the main targets of the Penguin series.

The vision behind the series was, therefore, to bring the classics to a very wide readership. Rieu himself had been a publisher by profession before embarking on his translation and editorial work; issues of sales and readership were rarely far from his thoughts. In a letter dated 9 February 1959 to Betty Radice, who was later to become his collaborator on the series and even later to succeed him as its editor, Rieu wrote: 'You mention the usefulness of the volumes in the series for classical teaching in schools and in reference libraries. We realise this – it is especially true of America. But it is not quite enough, when one has to sell

30,000 copies (at least) of each volume – a thought which intrudes itself whenever I am considering a new proposal.'[6]

The extent to which the phrase 'English-speaking readers' was wholly inclusive is shown by the following comment in a letter from Rieu to the Penguin office shortly after the publication of his *Iliad*: 'You will be amused to learn that the King has accepted the copy I sent him. His Secretary writes: "The King is already familiar with your admirable translation of the *Odyssey*, and looks forward to reading the *Iliad*." What a pity we must regard this as top secret' [16 April 1950]. Royalty was also at the head of the subscription list for Pope's *Odyssey*, but this similarity also shows up differences in approaches to both publishing and patronage.

V

In terms of the main lines of argument for translating poetry into prose as outlined in Section II above, Rieu's attitude seems to have been more negative than positive. It is true that the novel motif recurs in the introduction to the *Odyssey*:

> In form they [the *Iliad* and the *Odyssey*] are epic poems; but it will perhaps make their content clearer to the modern reader if I describe the *Iliad* as a tragedy and the *Odyssey* as a novel. It is in the *Iliad* that we hear for the first time the authentic voice of the Tragic Muse, while the *Odyssey*, with its well-knit plot, its psychological interest and its interplay of character, is the true ancestor of the long line of novels which have followed it.[7]

This affects his approach from and even at the outset: in the invocation at the start of book 1 of the *Odyssey* is a word which is normally translated as 'tell'; Rieu translates this as 'tell the tale of', and does so at some cost to the flow of his syntax.

But although he styles the *Iliad* as tragedy, he still translates it into prose. Also, the *Iliad* and the *Odyssey* are not the only poems Rieu translated into prose for the Penguin Classics series: Virgil's *Eclogues* received the same treatment, and here there is no possibility of maintaining an analogy with the novel form. In a characteristically terse note in his Introduction to the Virgil, Rieu wrote: 'Of the translation itself I will only say that it might well have been less like Virgil if I had laboured to render the music of

51

his hexameters in some traditional form of English verse. I have seen no attempt of the kind that has not lost more than it has gained by squeezing Virgil into a mould of alien design.'[8] This is a direct expression of Anne Dacier's concept of the lesser loss.

The kind of prose Rieu chose to use is determined by the aims of the Penguin Classics series. What it meant in practice is spelt out not by Rieu himself but by Betty Radice: 'To his translators his advice was simply "Write English" and "Read it aloud" as a test of whether the English written was natural, durable, and free from translationese, literary archaism and current slang. He had a sensitive ear for a well-turned sentence and read out every one of his own in order to get its "feel".'[9] This can be seen in relation to the translation tradition against which Rieu was reacting. But it may also be a response to the wider cultural values of the immediate post-war period as well. In an essay 'Politics and the English Language' published in the same year as Rieu's *Odyssey*, George Orwell writes about how political thought corrupts language and vice versa (a point he was to develop in the form of Newspeak in *Nineteen Eighty-Four*). His remedy is to draw up a set of rules which codify simplification:

   (i)   Never use a metaphor, simile, or other figure of speech which you are used to seeing in print.

  (ii)   Never use a long word where a short one will do.

 (iii)   If it is possible to cut out a word, always cut it out.

 (iv)   Never use the passive where you can use the active.

  (v)   Never use a foreign word, a scientific word, or a jargon word if you can think of an everyday English equivalent.

 (vi)   Break any of these rules sooner than say anything outright barbarous.

These tenets stand in the same relation to Rieu as Addison's to Pope (see Chapter 4, section 4). The main characteristics of his prose are short, plain words and short, plain sentences. The effects by which the Lang translations seek to achieve grandeur are avoided. This does not mean that it is without moments of occasional felicity: but these are mainly understated, and any phrase-making is in the idiom of the hymnal rather than the Bible. Here is his rendition of part of the sample passage from the start of *Odyssey* 11:

'Our first task, when we came down to the sea and reached our ship, was to run her into the good salt water and put the mast and sails on board. We then picked up the sheep we found there, and stowed them in the vessel. After which we ourselves embarked. And a melancholy crew we were. There was not a dry cheek in the company. However, Circe of the lovely tresses, human though she was in speech, proved her powers as a goddess by sending us the friendly escort of a favourable breeze, which sprang up from astern and filled the sail of our blue-prowed ship. All we had to do, after putting the tackle in order fore and aft, was to sit still, while the wind and the helmsman kept her straight. With a taut sail she forged ahead all day, till the sun went down and left her to pick her way through the darkness.'[10]

There is a further feature which distinguishes Rieu's version from most of the others, whether prose or verse. Homer, as we noted in Chapter 2, makes extensive use of speech, but without differentiating between narrative and speech or between characters. Rieu, however, seeks to draw a distinction between speech and other narrative: in one of his few critical comments he says of the speeches in the *Iliad* that 'They are forceful, logical and character-revealing to a high degree, but couched in so alien an idiom that if literally translated they sound pompous and silly'.[11] Thus, in representing characters' speech, in both poems, he extends his strategy of simplification by overlaying his short and plain diction with colloquialisms. Here is a sample chosen at random:

But the swineherd was most indignant. 'My good sir,' he exclaimed, 'what on earth put such a scheme into your head? You will simply be courting sudden death, if you insist on attaching yourself to a set of men whose profligacy and violence have outraged heaven itself. *Their* servants are not at all your kind, but smartly dressed young fellows, who always grease their hair and keep their pretty faces clean. That is the kind that wait on them – at polished tables, groaning under their load of bread and meat and wine. No, sir, stay with me, where nobody finds you a nuisance. I certainly don't, nor does any of my mates here. And when Odysseus' son arrives, he'll fit you out in a cloak and tunic and send you on wherever you would like to go.'[12]

This use of the oral idioms of Rieu's day has become the most striking feature of his translations in that it has the effect of dating them. It also results in something of a paradox: in seeking to avoid the overt anachronism of the Lang translations, he has produced a text which has dated more rapidly than them; Lang's recourse to the diction of the Authorized Version has given his translations a timelessness, Rieu's use of contemporary idiom is of its own time and no other.

VI

Perhaps, given the sales figures, we should expect that the early reception of Rieu's translations was highly favourable: however, this was not entirely the case. *Reynolds' News* in January 1946 wrote 'There is a new translation of the *Odyssey*, a very contemporary translation, and it costs one shilling. This is revolutionary... It is the *Odyssey* very much as a novel, still with the oceanic surge but without some of the thunder, almost colloquial but sinewy and of our own experience.'[13] A lengthy review in the *Times Literary Supplement* spelt out the reservations more fully:

> The vivacity and raciness of the Greek have been conveyed, and something also of the rapidity which Arnold put foremost of the qualities of Homer (though the rhythmic and controlled rapidity of the Homeric verse-form has, of necessity, vanished in prose). Perhaps, if there has to be a choice, this is the greater gain. We have laboured too long under a falsely statuesque conception of the Greeks; the Phidian aloofness, the embalmed and pedestalled perfection still need the iconoclastic hand.... But the hurt is there. Much of the nobility and much of the plain directness of ancient poetry has given way to the artifice of modern prose. Clarity and the ever-young story are there; but the incantation, the intoxicating freshness are in large measure gone.[14]

(The 'falsely statuesque conception of the Greeks' turns full circle on Swinburne's comments on Chapman's translation, quoted in Chapter 3, Section VI.)

More recent responses have been less kind. Adam Parry, son of Millman Parry whose work on the oral-formula theory of Homeric verse was mentioned in Chapter 2, Section I, wrote disparagingly:

> Rieu was the first to demonstrate beyond a doubt that Homer was really Anthony Trollope. As the editor and master spirit of the whole series of Penguin translations of Greek and Latin authors, Rieu can

stand as the Lang of the new style. The simple principle of the new style is that Homer really talked like us. There is of course a problem in deciding who we are. But even if we neglect this problem, we may find the assumption a little foolish.... The world of Homer is in fact vastly different from ours, different from the worlds of all of us, and to pretend that Homer talked as we do leads to translation as unreal as to pretend that he spoke – or composed – like the Jacobean translators of the Bible.[15]

Other writers have been even more dismissive, referring to Rieu's prose as 'cliché-ridden', 'excessively informal', 'devastatingly bathetic', and 'banal and vulgar'.[16]

Nevertheless Rieu does have his legacies within the tradition of Homeric translation, even if they are not necessarily ones he might have wished for.

Walter Shewring's prose translation of the *Odyssey* (1980) stands in the same position in relation to Rieu as Cowper does to Pope. In a lengthy 'Epilogue on Translation', Shewring mentions virtually every Homer translator other than Rieu. In this way Rieu is absent even from his own condemnation, because Shewring's strategy explicitly repudiates that of Rieu by undertaking to use 'words of the present century, but not the language of careless day-to-day talk and writing; a certain formality seems needful if the reader is to have some inkling of Homer's own much greater formality'. He refers scathingly to 'translators who assume in readers a general feeblemindedness and a deep distaste for serious language on serious matters, the more trivial word being thought more genuine.... This widespread technique – applied to the Bible or to Homer – degrades the writer while it insults the reader. Homer did not sing down to his audience.'[17]

Rieu's other legacy is that the mainstream has now moved back from translation from verse into prose to translation from verse into verse, as we shall see in the next chapter.

6

Christopher Logue's Translation: A Modernist Homer?

Contemporary translators of Homer now have little choice but to be conscious of the tradition of which they are seeking to become a part. Thus Christopher Logue writes in the Introduction to *War Music* (1981), one of his accounts of passages from Homer:

> Either the translations of the *Iliad* on which *War Music* is based did not exist or they had had only a passing interest for me until 1959 when Donald Carne-Ross suggested I contribute to a new version of the poem he was about to commission for the BBC.
>
> Knowing no Greek I began work on the passage he chose for me by studying the same passage in the translations published by Chapman (1611), Pope (1720), Lord Derby (1865), A. T. Murray (1924), and Rieu (1950).[1]

What is as significant as the names which are in Logue's personal tradition are the names which are not. Logue has set himself firmly in a line of poet-translators. He is consciously rejecting an alternative line of scholar-translators, of whom the most current and important at the time he was writing were the Americans Richmond Lattimore (*Iliad* (1951), *Odyssey* (1965)) and Robert Fitzgerald (*Odyssey* (1961), *Iliad* (1974)). In an interview in the summer of 1993 he stated:

> I look at new translations as they come out, that of Professors Knox and Fagles, for example, which is a touch sharper than Professor Lattimore's. However, these three professors may have been reading Homer all their lives, but he's failed to teach them what verse is. They do not write verse. They write blank-verse prose, sired by E. V. Rieu, via Lang, Leaf and Myers out of the King James Bible. It burbles

along but it doesn't scan. Still, such things make a bomb for the publishers.[2]

(Robert Fagles's version of the *Iliad* came out in 1990; his *Odyssey* in 1997.)

There is an implicit polarity, even animosity, here towards scholars and scholarship in the name of poetry; and this, too, is itself a feature of the tradition in which Logue is placing himself.

For example, we have already seen something of Chapman's animus against the 'grammarians merely and grammatical critics' from whom 'the divine rapture is most exempt' (see Chapter 3, Section III). We have also seen the scholar Bentley's criticism of the poet Pope's translations ('It is a pretty poem, Mr Pope, but you must not call it Homer' (see Chapter 4, Section II)). But Pope had his revenge, in a manner which was highly characteristic: much later he gave Bentley a leading role in an extended passage of the *Dunciad* (revised version of 1742/3; book IV, ll. 202–74), characterizing him as 'Thy mighty Scholiast, whose unweary'd pains | Made Horace dull and humbled Milton's strains'. He has his Bentley say: 'Turn what they will to Verse, their toil is vain, | Critics like me shall make it Prose again.' And E. V. Rieu's project, as we have seen, could be construed as anti-scholarly: even though his father was for many years a professor at University College, London, the few references to scholars in the Introduction to his *Odyssey* are, in their understated way, consistently negative.

II

This polarity is in some ways misleading. Of the three scholar-translators picked out (and picked on) by Logue, Lattimore and Fitzgerald have a body of poetry which is independent from their work as translators. Nevertheless it is important to understand the main characteristics of their translations of Homer in order to see the context in which – or, more accurately, against which – Logue sees himself as working.

The proliferation of complete translations of Homer in the post-war period, especially in America, is a striking phenomenon. In addition to those by Lattimore, Fitzgerald, and Fagles, there have been several others which are less well known in the

United Kingdom but of equal interest in terms of their approach and merits.[3] The publication of these numerous versions raises questions about demand and readership. Perhaps the spirit which prompted the extraordinary sales of Rieu's version is still abroad. More specifically, there might be an explanation in the massive growth of the higher education system in the United States in the late 1950s and early 1960s and the growing acceptance of classical civilization as an academic discipline, using translations rather than original texts as source material. Indeed, although, as we have seen, Rieu himself was working to an idea of the 'general reader' which went beyond an audience in schools and universities, his publishers had a conscious sales policy of targeting the American colleges market from as early as 1949.

Lattimore's is perhaps the most distinctive of these versions. His Homer is clearly heavily influenced by the contemporary work of Parry and his followers on Homer's oral formulae: in his Foreword to the *Iliad* he says that he has 'tried to preserve something of the formulaic character' but has 'not systematically attempted to render all identical passages in Greek by identical passages in English';[4] but overall few translators go to such lengths to reproduce Homer's repetitions. His translation is visibly different in that he has rejected the conventions on transliteration of names: Achilles appears as Achilleus, Hector as Hektor. Also he uses what he calls 'a free six-beat line', which is a longer line than most of the other contemporary translators, who mostly use a five-beat line and variations on it. But perhaps the most striking feature of Lattimore's translation, which he does not mention in his explanatory text, is that the content of each line in the English corresponds to the content of each line in the Greek: in its way this is a remarkable achievement, but the line as translation unit, coupled to Lattimore's scholarly approach, imposes great constraints on his scope to bring the order of ideas and phrases into line with contemporary usage. Here is a sample of his version of the *Iliad*:

> So he pondered, waiting, but Achilleus was closing upon him
> in the likeness of the lord of battles, the helm-shining warrior,
> and shaking from above his shoulder the dangerous Pelian
> ash spear, while the bronze that closed about him was shining
> like the flare of blazing fire or the sun in its rising.

And the shivers took hold of Hektor when he saw him, and he could no
    longer
stand his ground there, but left the gates behind, and fled, frightened,
and Peleus' son went after him in the confidence of his quick feet.

(Il. 22. 131–8)

In Silk's terminology, Lattimore achieves stylization without
immediacy. It was well received in its time, especially by fellow
scholar-translators. Robert Fitzgerald wrote of Lattimore's *Iliad*
that 'The feat is so decisive that it is reasonable to foresee a
century or so in which nobody will try again to put the *Iliad* in
English verse'. His own *Iliad* came out twenty-three years after
Lattimore's, and could be said to offer immediacy without
stylization. The formulaic element is played down, conjunctions
are stripped away. The emphasis is on rapidity:

> These were his shifts of mood. Now close at hand
> Achilles like the implacable god of war
> came on with blowing crest, hefting the dreaded
> beam of Pelian ash on his right shoulder.
> Bronze light played around him, like the glare
> of a great fire or the great sun rising,
> and Hector, as he watched, began to tremble.
> Then he could hold his ground no more. He ran,
> leaving the gate behind him, with Achilles
> hard on his heels, sure of his own speed.

The emphasis is also on rapidity in the versions by Robert
Fagles, which are strong on drama: a notable device which is a
distinguishing characteristic is his use of the dash as a means of
maintaining suspense and momentum simultaneously, as in this
passage:

> So he wavered,
> waiting there, but Achilles was closing on him now
> like the god of war, the fighter's helmet flashing,
> over his right shoulder shaking the Pelian ash spear,
> that terror, and the bronze around his body flared
> like a raging fire or the rising, blazing sun.
> Hector looked up, saw him, started to tremble,
> nerve gone, he could hold his ground no longer,
> he left the gates behind and away he fled in fear –
> and Achilles went for him, fast, sure of his speed...

(Il. 22. 156–65)

These translations take us back to the issue of the borderline between verse and prose. All three are free with the prosodic form they have set themselves: Fitzgerald, for example, seems to be aspiring to a five-beat line, but the overall metre is highly irregular. We have already seen Logue commenting that Lattimore and Fagles 'write blank-verse prose'. Two recent authors on Homer in translation have printed passages of Fitzgerald as prose: the line between his non-stylized poetry and the more stylized prose versions, such as that of Shewring discussed in Chapter 5, Section VI, is very narrow indeed.

Nevertheless, the end results are distinctively different from one another – which raises the question of how Logue can see them as a common enemy. An answer is perhaps given in the following passage:

> [Fluent translation strategies] take a characteristic form: they pursue linear syntax, univocal meaning or controlled ambiguity, current usage, linguistic consistency, conversational rhythms; they eschew unidiomatic constructions, polysemy, archaism, jargon, abrupt shifts in tone or diction, pronounced rhythmic regularity or sound repetitions – any textual effect, any play of the signifier, which calls attention to the materiality of language, to words as words, their opacity, their resistance to empathic response and interpretive mastery.[5]

This description fits collectively each of the individual approaches taken by Lattimore, Fitzgerald, and Fagles; and it is not difficult to see parallels with other aspects of the supposed American-led internationalization of culture.

III

Christopher Logue's own contribution to the English Homeric tradition has come in the form of a series of slim volumes containing versions of parts of the *Iliad*. *War Music* (covering books 16–19) appeared in 1981, *Kings* (books 1 and 2) in 1991, and *The Husbands* (books 3 and 4, 'plus material from books 2, 5, 7 and 11') in 1994. Even the choice to translate small gobbets, rather than complete books or the complete work, can be seen as its own rejection of the practices of the scholar-translators.

In each case formal publication followed the appearance of

earlier drafts, often in samizdat publications. This incremental publication history – which is reminiscent of the manner in which Chapman's Homer appeared – has been accompanied by gathering critical acclaim (from all save a few scholars). Possibly as a result, one can trace growing freedom in Logue's translation strategy over time, even to the point of overconfidence. In my own view the strengths of *War Music* are considerably diluted in the later volumes, and I shall be concentrating on the former.

Logue's is a modernist translation of Homer. Like uncovering the various layers of the historical Troy, it is possible to discern at least three overlapping but distinct layers of modernism in his versions.

The first is the direct influence of Ezra Pound, acknowledged in interviews. Logue's translation is an enactment of Pound's principles on translation as discussed in Chapter 1, Section II, in that it is conceived as a series of 'brilliant moments', both at the level of the individual phrase and in its overall architecture.

The second layer of modernism is more local. Logue first came to prominence in the 1960s and was involved with some of the more political and populist developments in the English poetry of the time, such as poster poetry; performance poetry and poetry and jazz; and anti-war protest poetry. Traces of each of these can be found in his Homer. As regards poster poetry, for example, in one place the word Apollo is printed in giant-sized capital letters across a double-page spread to suggest the god's grandeur and anger at the point where he decides to kill Patroclus. As regards performance poetry, parts of the work have been produced through media other than print, including radio, theatre, and disc. Thus the syntax is declamatory rather than periodic: as Logue once said in an interview, 'Poetry is not a silent art. The poem must perform unaided, in its reader's head'[6] – there are echoes here of Rieu's values, even if the outcomes are very different. Finally, and above all, *War Music* is acutely concerned with the violence and drama of war – this may be why Logue translates from the *Iliad* and not from the *Odyssey* – to the point where he could be misconstrued as glorifying it. But William Blake commented 'it is the Classics, & not Goths nor monks, that desolate Europe with wars';[7] and on this basis these concerns on Logue's part turn his reading of Homer into protest poetry.

The third layer of modernism is closer to postmodernism, an association – possibly deliberate, possibly an accident of contemporaneity – with the ideas of writers such as Derrida, which I discussed very briefly in Chapter 1. Thus, for example, Logue is not wedded to the source text–target text relationship. In the Introduction to *War Music*, as we have seen, he makes it clear to the reader that he knows no Greek himself, that he has worked from previous translations and a prose crib of the original, and, moreover, that he is unashamed of this. He is not even wedded to the sanctity of text itself. His is a multimedia *Iliad*, which makes particular use of contemporary visual stylistics: in places this is explicit, as in metaphors such as 'Cut to the fleet' or 'Jump cuts like these...'; in other places it is implicit, as when he describes the plain of Troy as if using a panning shot or when, in a cinematic cliché, Patroclus, struggling to stay alive, grasps an ankle, looks slowly up the body attached, and sees Hector looking down at him. These devices directly parallel Pope's allusions to contemporary visual aesthetics in his text and commentary, as described in Chapter 4, Section III.

Nor, unlike the other translators we have looked at, is Logue closely wedded to Homer. Extreme, deliberate, and ostentatious departure from the source text pervades his work at all levels. The vocabulary he uses includes frequent examples of overt anachronisms: *War Music* features cars, planes, yachts, rockets at Cape Kennedy, pistons, trampolines, windcheaters, vampires, radium, and tungsten, and more besides. *Kings* features by way of a simile a snapshot of Logue himself and friends in the city of Skopje shortly before it was destroyed by an earthquake. (Such time-travelling collage is not new. Basil Bunting, another Pound acolyte, produced translations of the medieval French poet François Villon peopled by, among others, General Grant, General Lee, and Florence Nightingale.)

Moreover, this is only a small-scale manifestation of an overall effect. In fact, Logue's divergence from his source text is so extreme that it is easier to enumerate the similarities. It is possible to find some resemblance to the order of events in Homer, especially in some parts of *War Music* and in the translation of *Iliad 21*, Achilles' fight with the river Scamander (available only in anthology). He also makes extensive use of epic similes, even if the similes he uses are not always close to those Homer uses. Some of the other Homeric features have also survived, such as set-piece speeches. There is a divine machinery, even if what the gods and goddesses say and do is, again, not always as in Homer.

Other features, however, have not survived. Most conspicuously, as Logue states in his introduction to *War Music*, he has decided '(mostly) to omit Homer's descriptive epithets, "ten-second-miler-Achilles", "thick-as-a-pyramid-Ajax" and so forth',[8] thus at a stroke resolving an issue which has been the source of much concern to other more conscientious translators, especially in this period. What Logue does not mention here is that he also (mostly) omits all other forms of formulaic repetition – not just the noun-phrase epithet but also the formulae in the form of a verse or a block of verses and other more indirect forms of repetition.

Logue also compresses and amplifies text at will (or at whim). Speech, which, as we saw in Chapter 2, Section III, even Pound, Logue's hero and mentor, mentioned as one of Homer's great graces, is almost always compressed in Logue. For example, in a scene which in Homer comes towards the end of *Iliad* 16, the dying Patroclus has taunted Hector with the threat of death at the hands of Achilles. In a word-for-word translation the original reads something like the following:

> Even as Patroclus was speaking the end of death covered him; and his soul flying from his limbs was gone to Hades, bewailing its fate, leaving manliness and youth behind. And even as he died glorious Hector spoke to him: 'Patroclus, why do you prophesy for me sudden, total destruction? Who knows whether Achilles, son of fair-haired Thetis, may be struck by my spear first and lose his life?' So saying, he pulled the bronze spear out of the wound, setting his foot on the body, and pushed it backwards from the spear.[9]

Logue translates this as follows:

> Saying these things Patroclus died.
> And as his soul went through the sand
> Hector withdrew his spear and said
> 'Perhaps.'

Logue's version here is representative of the daring way in which he compresses speech. With the epic simile, by contrast, whether they are based in Homer's original or of his own invention, his tendency is towards expansion. Also, he is even more explicit than Homer in his descriptions of violence.

Compression and amplification are also carried out on a larger scale. Whole sections of the original are omitted. Thus, for example, in Logue's account of book 18, after Patroclus' body has been taken back by the Greeks, a debate in the Trojan camp and the description of the making of Achilles' Shield are simply omitted. Material is organized: thus, instead of rendering Homer's somewhat chaotic battle scenes in full, Logue uses various devices to shape them, including editorialization – 'Of several incidents, consider two'. And material is even added, although much less so in *War Music* than in the more recent books.

IV

Clearly Logue's approach raises the question of the point at which a 'translation' turns into a 'paraphrase' or 'free imitation' under Steiner's 'sterile triadic model' (see Chapter 1, Section II) – are the liberties he takes too great for the end result to be regarded as a reflection of Homer? But, for all the divergence, there is still plenty of Homeric material in Logue. To put the question from the other side, if categorization is necessary, Logue's Homer could not be regarded as coming into the category of works which use the mythic core of Homer and nothing more, such as Joyce's *Ulysses* or Walcott's *Omeros*. But it is also arguable that in some ways Logue's Homer is more faithful as a translation than other more apparently 'faithful' versions such as those I discussed in the earlier part of this chapter.

Using again Silk's formulation of immediacy and stylization as the essential characteristics of Homer's style, there can be little doubt that Logue's Homer is immediate – much more so than Lattimore and Fitzgerald and possibly even than Fagles.

Silk's concept of stylization, however, raises more complex issues. The American scholar-translators, arguably, have discarded stylization in favour of fluent translation strategies. We have also seen how Logue has discarded most of the devices which give Homer his stylization. Nevertheless, his version undoubtedly has a substitute stylization of its own. This has three main characteristics, none of which has any root in the Homeric 'original'.

The first is in his creation of atmosphere, by a technique which is close to verbal impressionism. Here is Logue's version of the famous 'rosy-fingered Dawn' formula, with only a fingerhold on the Greek text:

> Rat.
> Pearl.
> Onion.
> Honey:
> These colours came before the Sun
> Lifted above the ocean,
> Bringing light
> Alike to mortals and Immortals.[10]

This demands that we imagine for ourselves the slow growth of daybreak through a spectrum of shades of light and colour: which leads in turn to a second aspect of Logue's stylization – namely, a reflective complicity between writer and reader. We have already discussed his use of visualization, including techniques from film: but what is striking is the extent to which Logue demands the reader's involvement in this process, with repeated verbs of seeing or imagining, often as imperatives or close equivalents, especially at the beginning of similes – 'Imagine wolves', 'Picture a canted yacht at speed', 'Now I must ask you to forget reality', 'Now I shall ask you to imagine how | Men under discipline of death prepare for war', and many others. We become Logue's accomplices in feeling the atmosphere and watching the action, his conspirators in the translatorial freedom he has given himself.

The third characteristic is architectural. In *War Music* the passages of the *Iliad* he chooses to cover are presented as rounded self-contained episodes, rather than as part of Auerbach's 'continuous foreground'; and each ends on a note of grimly ironic prophecy, as with Hector's 'Perhaps' which I quoted earlier. This procedure is rooted in an ostentatious exercise of the artist's right to select; and it also contributes to the motif of brief intensity which underpins the conception of his work as a whole.

Even more than atmospheric impressionism or complicity between author and reader, brief intensity contradicts much of our understanding of epic architectonics: so how can Logue's work be called a translation of Homer? There is a theoretical framework which goes some way towards answering this question. In a joint article on the current state of translation studies written in 1990, Lefevre and Bassnett, two of the most influential of the thinkers and writers currently working in this field, advance the idea of 'cultural reality... the way literature operates in a culture in this day and age'. Logue's use of visual techniques can be seen as an example of this: visual media such as cinema and television are as much a part of our cultural reality as literary texts, possibly more so; and for Logue they are both competition and challenge of a kind previous translators never had. But Lefevre and Bassnett also have a deeper meaning for their idea in its relation to translation:

> Literature reaches those who are not its professional students much more by way of the 'images' constructed of it in translations, but even more so in anthologies, commentaries, histories and, occasionally, critical journals, than it does so by means of 'originals', however venerable they may be... What impacts most on members of a culture, we suggest, is the 'image' of a work of literature, not its 'reality', not the text that is still sacrosanct only in literature departments.[11]

While Logue's approach, both close-up and on a wide-angled lens, may indeed go against much of our understanding of epic technique and architectonics, 'cultural reality' may now make it impossible for full-scale Homeric epic ever to be realized for the general reader at the end of the twentieth century. In spite of this, Logue is still seeking to convey what he sees as the poetic in Homer: and the risks he takes enable him to go further in this direction than the safer strategies of those he sees as his rivals.

The passage from the *Iliad* which I have been using in previous chapters is not covered in Logue's selective readings from Homer. Here, instead, is a passage from Achilles' fight with the river Scamander in Book 21:

> Hearing this
> The Greek jumped clear into the water and Scamander
> Went for him in hatred: curved back his undertow, and
> Hunched like a snarling yellow bull drove the dead up
> And out, tossed by the water's snout on to the fields,
> Yet those who lived he hid behind a gentle wave.

Around the Greek Scamander deepened. Wave clambered
Over wave to get at him, beating aside his studded shield so,
Both footholds gone, half toppled over by the bloodstained crud,
Achilles snatched for balance at an elm – ah! – its roots gave –
Wrenched out – splitting the bank, and tree and all
Crashed square across the river; leaves, splintered branches
And dead birds, blocking the fall. Then Achilles wanted out.
And scrambled through the root's lopsided crown, out of the ditch,
Off home.

    But the river Scamander had not done with him.
Forcing its bank, an avid lip of water slid
After him, to smother his Greek breath for Trojan victory.
Aoi! – but that Greek could run! – and put and kept
A spearthrow's lead between him and the quick,
Suck, quick, curve of the oncoming water,
Arms outstretched as if to haul himself along the air,
His shield – like the early moon – thudding against
His nape-neck and his arse, fast, fast
As the black winged hawk's full stoop he went –
And what is faster? – yet, Scamander was nigh on him,
Its hood of seething water poised over his shoulderblades.
Achilles was a quick man, yes, but the gods are quicker than men.
And easily Scamander's wet webbed claw stroked his ankles.

    You must imagine how a gardener prepares
    To let his stored rainwater out, along
    The fitted trench to nourish his best plants.
    Carefully, with a spade, he lifts the stone
    Gagging the throat of his trench, inch by inch,
    And, as the water flows, pebbles, dead grubs,
    Old bits of root and dusts are gathered and
    Swept along by the speed of it, until
    Singing among the plants, the bright water
    Overtakes its gardener and his control
    Is lost. Likewise Scamander took Achilles.[12]

V

Current opinion on Logue divides very much along predictable
lines. George Steiner, writing from a theoretical perspective,
calls Logue's 'fragments' 'an act of genius', '"translation"
blazing into great poetry'.[13] Bernard Knox, a classical scholar
mentioned in one of the quotations from Logue at the start of

this chapter, regards much of Logue's strategy as 'trivialisation' and 'downgrading'; and in an echo of the criticism directed fifty years earlier at Rieu, draws attention to what he sees as its vulgarity and sensationalism.[14]

In previous chapters we have seen how the reputations of the various translations we have been looking at have reached heights and depths, often within remarkably short spaces of time; and it is reasonable to assume that in time Logue's version will seem as dated as that of Rieu. One of the points on which Rieu would agree with Lang, whom otherwise he seeks to supplant, concerns the temporal relativity and impermanence of translations: Betty Radice quotes Rieu as saying that 'every generation should re-examine its interpretation of the classics'; while Lang begins the Preface to the *Odyssey* he translated with Butcher with the following declaration: 'There would have been less controversy about the proper method of Homeric translation, if critics had recognised that the question is a purely relative one, that of Homer there can be no final translation. The taste and the literary habits of each age demand different qualities in poetry, and therefore a different sort of rendering of Homer.'[15]

Similarly the taste and literary habits of each reader: which is why I do not intend to end this book with my own selection of preferred translations. I hope, instead, that I have given readers a fuller idea of factors to take into account in making that decision for themselves.

Notes

CHAPTER 1.   TRANSLATION: SOME ISSUES

1. See E. Gentzler, *Contemporary Translation Theories* (London, 1993), chs. 3 and 4, for a useful summary of the main lines of argument in these various areas.
2. V. Nabokov, 'Problems of Translation: *Onegin* in English', *Partisan Review*, 22 (1955), 504, 510, 512.
3. Quoted in H. Kenner, *The Pound Era* (London, 1972), 147–53.
4. Translation for the stage in P. Arnott, 'Greek Drama and the Modern Stage', in W. Arrowsmith and R. Shattuck (eds.), *The Craft and Context of Translation* (Austin, Tex.: 1961), 83–94; translation for the audience in A. Sommerstein, 'On Translating Aristophanes: Ends and Means', *Greece & Rome*, 20 (1973), 140–54; 'textual organicity' in J. Delisle, *Translation: An Interpretive Approach* (Ottawa, 1988); 'an inventory of competences' in A. Lefevre, *Translating Poetry: Seven Strategies and a Blueprint* (Amsterdam, 1975).
5. I. A. Richards, 'Towards a Theory of Translating', in A. F. Wright (ed.), *Studies in Chinese Thought* (Chicago, Ill.: 1953), 247–62.
6. G. Steiner, *After Babel* (Oxford, new edn., 1992), 319.
7. There is a clear account of Derrida's ideas on translation in Gentzler, *Contemporary Translation Theories*, ch. 6.
8. Steiner, *After Babel*, 370.
9. Homer, trans. R. Fagles, *The Iliad* (Harmondsworth, 1990); Levi quote on back cover.

CHAPTER 2.   TRANSLATING HOMER: SOME ISSUES

1. R. Janko, 'Thunder but no Clouds: The Genesis of the Homeric Text', *Didaskalia* (Winter 1996), no page numbers – electronic journal.

2. For a summary of the latest views with full supporting bibliography, see R. Rutherford, 'Homer', *Greece & Rome: New Surveys in the Classics*, 26 (1996).

3. E. S. Sherratt, '"Reading the Texts": Archaeology and the Homeric Question', in C. Emlyn-Jones, L. Hardwick, and J. Purkis (eds.), *Homer: Readings and Images* (London, 1992), 145–65.

4. E. Auerbach, *Mimesis: The Representation of Reality in Western Literature* (Princeton, NJ, 1953), 6–7.

5. Longinus, *On the Sublime*, ch. 9 in T. S. Dorsch (ed. and trans.), *Classical Literary Criticism* (Harmondsworth, 1986), 111.

6. Cited in J. Barnes, *Early Greek Philosophy* (Harmondsworth, 1987), 95.

7. E. Cantarella, *Pandora's Daughters: The Role and Status of Women in Greek and Roman Antiquity* (Baltimore, Md., 1987), 33; quoted in C. D. Williams, *Pope, Homer, and Manliness* (London, 1993), 116–17.

8. M. Arnold, 'On Translating Homer', in *On the Classical Tradition: The Complete Prose Works of Matthew Arnold*, i (Ann Arbor, Mich., 1960), 102.

9. M. Silk, *The Iliad* (Landmarks of World Literature; Cambridge, 1987), 54–69.

10. W. A. Camps, *An Introduction to Homer* (Oxford, 1980), 17.

11. E. Pound, 'Translators of Greek: Early Translators of Homer', in T. S. Eliot (ed.), *Literary Essays of Ezra Pound* (London, 1960), 250.

12. Based on A. T. Murray's Loeb translation (1924–5), with some vocabulary modernized and changes of word order.

13. A. T. Murray in the Loeb edition (1919), Butcher and Lang (1867), Cowper (1791), Lattimore (1965), Pope (1725), Rieu (1946), Rouse (1937), T. E. Shaw (1932), and Shewring (1980) respectively.

CHAPTER 3.   GEORGE CHAPMAN'S TRANSLATION: AN ELIZABETHAN HOMER?

1. R. Fagles, 'Homer and the Writers', in G. Steiner and R. Fagles (eds.), *Homer: A Collection of Critical Essays* (Englewood Cliffs, NJ, 1962), 160.

2. Although it should be said that less than ten copies of it survive and that only very small amounts have been reproduced from these in anthologies.

3. H. Wright, *The Life and Works of Arthur Hall of Grantham, Member of Parliament, Courtier and First Translator of Homer into English* (Manchester, 1919), 160.

4. J. Willcox, 'Ficino's Commentary on Plato's *Ion* and Chapman's

Inspired Poet in the *Odyssey'*, *Philological Quarterly*, 64/1 (1985), 198.
5. Commentarius to book 1.
6. This passage is the source of its own separate literary tradition, of which the most notable recent example is Auden's poem 'The Shield of Achilles' (1952).
7. The artist in J. Krasner, '*The Tragedy of Bussy D'Ambois* and the Creation of Heroism', *Medieval and Renaissance Drama*, 4 (1989), 107–21; the psychological mode in R. Sowerby, 'Chapman's Discovery of Homer', *Translation and Literature*, 1 (1992), 26–51.
8. G. de F. Lord, *Homeric Renaissance: The 'Odyssey' of George Chapman* (London, 1956), 39 and 41.
9. 'Vail' in the fourth line is possibly used here in the archaic sense of doffing headgear as a mark of respect.
10. S. Johnson, *Lives of the English Poets: A Selection* (London, 1975), 331.
11. Cited in E. T. Webb (ed.), *English Romantic Hellenism 1700–1824* (Manchester, 1982), 210.
12. M. Arnold, 'On Translating Homer', in *On the Classical Tradition: The Complete Prose Works of Matthew Arnold*, i (Ann Arbor, Mich., 1960), 113.
13. A. C. Swinburne, *George Chapman: A Critical Essay* (London, 1875), 6.
14. T. S. Eliot, 'The Metaphysical Poets', in *Selected Prose* (London, 1953), 116.
15. G. Snare, *The Mystification of George Chapman* (Durham and London, 1989).

CHAPTER 4. ALEXANDER POPE'S TRANSLATION: AN AUGUSTAN HOMER?

1. Whatever their success in literary terms, they certainly did well financially. Johnson reports that Pope received £5,320 4s. from the subscription and linked arrangements with the publisher for the *Iliad* and a smaller but 'still very considerable amount' for the *Odyssey*; Pope's own figures, as reported to his friend Spence, were £1,200 and £600 respectively. By contrast, he had received £7 for 'The Rape of the Lock' in its original form and a further £15 for it in its expanded form.
2. See K. Simonsuuri, *Homer's Original Genius: Eighteenth-Century Notions of the Early Greek Epic 1688–1798* (Cambridge, 1979), 19–64.
3. C. D. Williams, *Pope, Homer, and Manliness* (London, 1993), 43.
4. *Twickenham Edition of the Poems of Alexander Pope* (London, 1967), vii. 23.
5. S. Shankman, *Pope's 'Iliad': Homer in the Age of Passion* (Princeton,

NJ, 1983), 82.

6. S. Johnson, *Lives of the English Poets: A Selection* (London, 1975), 329.

7. M. Hodgart, 'The Subscription List for Pope's *Iliad*', in R. B. White (ed.) *The Dress of Words: Essays in Restoration and Eighteenth Century Literature in Honour of Richmond P. Bond* (Lawrence, Kan., 1978), 25–34.

8. G. Sherburn (ed.), *The Correspondence of Alexander Pope* (Oxford, 1956), i. 208–9.

9. J. Spence, *Anecdotes, Observations and Characters of Books and Men* (Oxford, 1966), i. 82–3.

10. Sherburn, *Correspondence*, ii. 341.

11. Ibid.

12. Johnson, *Lives*, 331.

13. *Twickenham Edition*, vii, 18.

14. Pope's footnote here includes the comment, 'A painter might form from this passage the picture of Mars in the fullness of his terrors, as well as Phidias is said to have drawn from another, that of Jupiter in all his majesty.'

15. Shankman, *Pope's 'Iliad'*.

16. *Twickenham Edition*, vii. 4.

17. *Idler*, 77, written in 1759.

18. Johnson, *Lives*, 394, 333, and 395.

19. Quoted in E. T. Webb (ed.), *English Romantic Hellenism 1700–1824* (Manchester, 1982), 176 and 179.

20. Quoted in Shankman, *Pope's 'Iliad'*, 99–100.

21. M. Arnold, 'On Translating Homer', in *On the Classical Tradition: The Complete Prose Works of Matthew Arnold*, i (Ann Arbor, Mich., 1960), 111.

CHAPTER 5. E. V. RIEU'S TRANSLATION: A MODERN HOMER?

1. G. Steiner, *Poem into Poem: World Poetry in Modern Verse Translation* (Harmondsworth, 1970), 21.

2. K. Simonsuuri, *Homer's Original Genius: Eighteenth Century Notions of the Early Greek Epic 1688–1798* (Cambridge, 1979), 52.

3. S. Butcher and A. Lang, *The Odyssey* (London, 1879).

4. *The Notebooks of Samuel Butler* (London, 1985), 197.

5. E. V. Rieu, *The Odyssey* (Harmondsworth, 1946), p. xix.

6. Previously unpublished letter in the Penguin archive, Special Collections, Bristol University Library.

7. Rieu, *The Odyssey*, p. viii.

8. E. V. Rieu, *Virgil: The Pastoral Poems* (Harmondsworth, 1949), 17.
9. B. Radice, 'A Classic Education', *The Times Higher Education Supplement*, 19 Oct. 1984, 17.
10. Rieu, *The Odyssey*, 175.
11. E. V. Rieu, 'The Faith of a Translator', in Penguin Collectors' Society, *Miscellany 9: The Penguin Classics* (June 1994), 32.
12. Rieu, *The Odyssey*, 246.
13. Quoted in *Miscellany 9*, 6.
14. Anon., 'The Homeric Dilemma: Overhauling the English Translations', *The Times Literary Supplement*, 23 Mar. 1946, 138.
15. A. Parry, 'What Can We Do to Homer?', in *The Language of Achilles and Other Papers* (Oxford, 1989), 42–3.
16. Respectively D. Carne-Ross, 'Homer', *Arion*, 7/3 (Autumn 1968), 406; R. Rutherford, 'Homer', *Greece & Rome: New Surveys in the Classics*, 106; M. S. Silk, *Journal of the Hellenic Society*, 110 (1990), 205; and H. A. Mason, *To Homer through Pope: An Introduction to Homer's 'Iliad' and Pope's Translation* (London, 1972), 186.
17. W. Shewring, *The Odyssey* (Oxford, 1980), 313–14.

CHAPTER 6.   CHRISTOPHER LOGUE'S TRANSLATION: A MODERNIST HOMER?

1. C. Logue, *War Music* (London, 1981), 7. Lord Derby was Prime Minister three times in the 1850s and 1860s; his *Iliad* was published in 1864. A. T. Murray produced the translation for the Loeb Classical Library edition of Homer (Cambridge, Mass., *Odyssey* 1919; *Iliad* 1924).
2. (C. Logue), 'The Art of Poetry LXVI (Interview)' *Paris Review*, 127 (Summer 1993), 254.
3. For example, those by Ennis Rees (*Odyssey* (1960)) and Allen Mandlebaum (*Odyssey* (1990)).   *mandelbaum*
4. R. Lattimore, *The Iliad of Homer* (Chicago, 1951), 7.
5. L. Venuti, 'Introduction', in L. Venuti (ed.), *Rethinking Translation: Discourse, Subjectivity, Ideology* (London, 1992), 4.
6. *Paris Review*, 257.
7. E. T. Webb (ed.), *English Romantic Hellenism 1700–1824* (Manchester, 1982), 28. A fuller contemporary exploration of these ideas can be found in Simone Weil's essay 'The *Iliad*, Poem of Might', in *Intimations of Christianity among the Ancient Greeks* (London, 1957), 24–55: 'The true hero,' she writes, 'the real subject, the core of the *Iliad*, is might. That which is wielded by men rules over it, and before it man's flesh cringes.'

8. Logue, *War Music*, 7.
9. Murray's Loeb translation, modernized.
10. Logue, *War Music*, 68.
11. A. Lefevre and S. Bassnett, 'Introduction: Proust's Grandmother and the Thousand and One Nights: The "Cultural Turn" in Translation Studies', in S. Bassnett and A. Lefevre (eds.), *Translation, History and Culture* (London, 1990), 9–10.
12. C. Logue, *Selected Poems* (London, 1996), 136–7; full passage 134–41. The same extract appears, with minor differences, in two Penguin anthologies, E. Lucie-Smith (ed.), *British Poetry since 1945* (Harmondsworth, 1970), 295–302 and D. Wright (ed.), *The Mid Century: English Poetry 1940–1960* (Harmondsworth, 1965), 220–7.
13. G. Steiner and A. Dykman (eds.), *Homer in English* (Harmondsworth, 1996), 298.
14. B. Knox, 'Homeroidal', *London Review of Books*, 11 May 1995, 23.
15. This is, the reader will recall, the introduction to a *prose* translation.

Select Bibliography

ANTHOLOGIES

Poole, A., and Maule, J. (eds.), *The Oxford Book of Classical Verse in Translation* (Oxford, 1995). Sixty-one pages of extracts of various translations of Homer, including generous helpings of Chapman and Logue.

Steiner, G. (ed.), *Poem into Poem: World Poetry in Modern Verse Translation* (Harmondsworth, 1970).

—— and Dykman, A. (eds.), *Homer in English* (Harmondsworth, 1996). Chronological, with short accounts of each author. Twenty-seven pages of selections from Chapman.

Tomlinson, C. (ed.), *The Oxford Book of Verse in English Translation* (Oxford, 1980).

TRANSLATION THEORY

Arnott, P., 'Greek Drama and the Modern Stage', in W. Arrowsmith and R. Shattuck (eds.), *The Craft and Context of Translation* (Austin, Tex., 1961), 83–94.

Benjamin, W., 'The Task of the Translator', in *Illuminations* (London, 1972), 70–82.

Delisle, J., *Translation: An Interpretive Approach* (Ottawa, 1988).

Derrida, J., 'Des Tours de Babel', in J. F. Graham (ed.), *Difference in Translation* (Ithaca, NY, 1985), 165–207.

Gentzler, E. J., *Contemporary Translation Theories* (London, 1993). Clear and valuable as a starting point for twentieth-century thinking on translation.

Kelly, L. G., *The True Interpreter: A History of Translation Theory and Practice in the West* (Oxford, 1979). Valuable as a starting point for pre-twentieth-century thinking on translation.

75

Lefevre, A., *Translating Poetry: Seven Strategies and a Blueprint* (Amsterdam, 1975).

―――― *Translation/History/Culture: A Sourcebook* (London, 1992).

―――― and Bassnett, S., 'Introduction: Proust's Grandmother and the Thousand and One Nights: The "Cultural Turn" in Translation Studies', in S. Bassnett and A. Lefevre (eds.), *Translation, History and Culture* (London, 1990), 1–13.

Nabokov, V., 'Problems of Translation: *Onegin* in English', *Partisan Review*, 22 (1955), 496–512.

Richards, I. A., 'Towards a Theory of Translating', in A. F. Wright (ed.), *Studies in Chinese Thought* (Chicago, 1953), 247–62.

Sommerstein, A., 'On Translating Aristophanes: Ends and Means', *Greece & Rome*, 20 (1973), 140–54.

✓ Steiner, G., *After Babel* (Oxford, new edn., 1992). Challenging; not an easy read, but the rewards are great.

Venuti, L., 'Introduction', in L. Venuti (ed.), *Rethinking Translation: Discourse, Subjectivity, Ideology* (London, 1992).

HOMERIC AND OTHER CLASSICAL STUDIES

There is an enormous literature on Homer. This is a short, personal selection, which includes bibliographies for further reading as indicated.

✓ Auerbach, E., *Mimesis: The Representation of Reality in Western Literature* (1946; Princeton, NJ, 1953). See especially Chapter 1.

Camps, W. A., *An Introduction to Homer* (Oxford, 1980).

Cantarella, E., *Pandora's Daughters: The Role and Status of Women in Greek and Roman Antiquity* (Baltimore, Md., 1987).

Morris, I., and Powell, B., *A New Companion to Homer* (Leiden, 1997). State-of-the-art scholarship, with extensive bibliography.

Rutherford, R., 'Homer', *Greece & Rome: New Surveys in the Classics*, 26 (1996). Particularly useful as a supporting bibliography.

Sherratt, E. S., '"Reading the Texts": Archaeology and the Homeric Question', in C. Emlyn-Jones, L. Hardwick, and J. Purkis (eds.), *Homer: Readings and Images* (London, 1992), 145–65. This is an Open University course book and as such is very accessible to the non-specialist.

Silk, M., *The Iliad* (Landmarks of World Literature; Cambridge, 1987). Short, very readable introduction for non-specialists, with short annotated bibliography.

✓ Steiner, G., and Fagles, R. *Homer: A Collection of Critical Essays* (Englewood Cliffs, NJ, 1962). Interesting literary meta-commentaries on Homer.

Weil, S., 'The *Iliad*, Poem of Might', in *Intimations of Christianity among the Ancient Greeks* (London, 1957), 24–55.

GEORGE CHAPMAN

Briggs, J. C., 'Chapman's *Seaven Bookes of the Iliades*: Mirror for Essex', *Studies in English Literature 1500–1900*, 21 (1981), 59–73.

Fay, H. C., 'Poetry, Pedantry, and Life in Chapman's *Iliads*', *Review of English Studies* NS 4/13 (1953), 13–25.

Lord, G. de F., *Homeric Renaissance: The 'Odyssey' of George Chapman* (London, 1956).

MacLure, M., *George Chapman: A Critical Study* (Toronto, 1966). Useful general introduction, which also places Chapman's translations in the context of his other works.

Sowerby, R., 'Chapman's Discovery of Homer', *Translation and Literature*, 1 (1992), 26–51. Another useful starting point.

Snare, G., *The Mystification of George Chapman* (Durham and London, 1989).

Swinburne, A. C., *George Chapman: A Critical Essay* (London, 1875).

Willcox, J. F., 'Ficino's Commentary on Plato's *Ion* and Chapman's Inspired Poet in the *Odyssey*', *Philological Quarterly*, 64/1 (1985), 198.

ALEXANDER POPE

Brower, R., 'Pope's *Iliad* for Twentieth-Century Readers', in *Mirror on Mirror: Translation, Imitation and Parody* (Cambridge, Mass.: 1974), 55–76.

Crossley, R., 'Pope's *Iliad*: The Commentary and the Translation', *Philological Quarterly* 56 (1977), 339–57.

Hodgart, M., 'The Subscription List for Pope's *Iliad*', in R. B. White Jnr. (ed.), *The Dress of Words: Essays in Restoration and Eighteenth Century Literature in Honour of Richmond P. Bond* (Lawrence, Kan., 1978), 25–34.

Johnson, S., *Life of Pope* (1781), in *Lives of the English Poets: A Selection* (London, 1975), 315–415.

Knight, D., *Pope and the Heroic Tradition* (New Haven, Conn., 1951).

Mack, M. *et al.*, 'Introduction', *Twickenham Edition of the Poems of Alexander Pope*, vii–viii. *The Iliad*, ix–x. *The Odyssey* (London, 1967), vii pp. xxxv–ccxlix. Thorough and informative.

Mason, H. A., *To Homer through Pope: An Introduction to Homer's 'Iliad' and Pope's Translation* (London, 1972), Idiosyncratic and stimulating.

Russo, J. P., 'Homer and the Heroic Ideal', in *Alexander Pope: Tradition and Identity* (Cambridge, Mass., 1972), 83–132. Another good starting-point.

Shankman, S., *Pope's 'Iliad': Homer in the Age of Passion* (Princeton, NJ, 1983).

Sherburn, G., *The Correspondence of Alexander Pope* (Oxford, 1956).

Simonsuuri, K., *Homer's Original Genius: Eighteenth-Century Notions of the Early Greek Epic 1688–1798* (Cambridge, 1979).

Spence, J., *Anecdotes, Observations and Characters of Books and Men* (Oxford, 1966).

Staves, S., 'Pope's Refinement', in B. Hammond (ed.), *Pope* (Longman's Critical Readers; London, 1996), 26–40.

Williams, C. D., *Pope, Homer, and Manliness* (London, 1993). A reading which seeks to draw out gender issues.

E. V. RIEU AND OTHER PROSE TRANSLATIONS

Anon., 'The Homeric Dilemma: Overhauling the English Translations', *The Times Literary Supplement*, 23 Mar. 1946, 138.

Carne-Ross, D. 'Homer', *Arion*, 7/3 (Autumn 1968), 400–8.

Hare, S. (ed.), *Allen Lane and the Penguin Editors 1935–1970* (London, 1995), 186–90.

Radice, B., 'A Classic Education', *The Times Higher Education Supplement*, 19 Oct. 1984, 17.

Rieu, E. V., 'The Faith of a Translator', in Penguin Collectors' Society, *Miscellany 9: The Penguin Classics* (June 1994), 32–3.

CHRISTOPHER LOGUE AND OTHER POST-WAR VERSE TRANSLATIONS

Bagg, R., 'Translating the Abyss: On Robert Fitzgerald's *Odyssey*', *Arion*, 8/1 (Spring 1969), 51–65.

Carne-Ross, D., 'Structural Translation: Notes on Logue's *Patrokleia*', *Arion*, 1/2 (Summer 1962), 27–38.

Fitzgerald, R., 'Postscript to a Translation of the *Odyssey*', in W. Arrowsmith and R. Shattuck (eds.), *The Craft and Context of Translation* (New York, 1964; not in the 1961 University of Texas Press edition), 303–51.

Knox, B., 'Homeroidal', *London Review of Books*, 11 May 1995, 23.

Lattimore, R., 'Practical Notes on Translating Greek Poetry' in Reuben A. Brower (ed.), *On Translating* (Cambridge, Mass., 1959), 48–56.

(Logue, C.), 'The Art of Poetry LXVI (Interview)', *Paris Review*, 127 (Summer 1993), 238–64.

—— 'Interview with Christopher Logue', *Thumbscrew*, 1 (Winter 1994–5), 15–23.

COMPARATIVE CRITICISM AND OTHER USEFUL ITEMS

Arnold, M., 'On Translating Homer', in *On the Classical Tradition: The Complete Prose Works of Matthew Arnold*, i (Ann Arbor, Mich., 1960). ✓

Butler, S., *The Authoress of the 'Odyssey'* (London, 1922; repr. Chicago, 1967).

Clarke, H., *Homer's Readers* (Newark, Del., 1981). Interesting account of varying readings of Homer over time; opening chapter on the medieval tradition particularly useful.

Cohen, J. M., *English Translators and Translations* (London, 1962). ✓

Lloyd-Jones, H., 'Translating Homer', in *Greek in a Cold Climate* (London, 1991), 1–17. Comparative, focusing mainly on Fagles.

Ogilivie, R. M., *Latin and Greek: A History of the Influence of the Classics on English Life from 1600 to 1918* (London, 1964).

Parry, A., 'What Can We Do to Homer?', in *The Language of Achilles and Other Papers* (Oxford, 1989), 39–49. Comparative, mainly Rieu and Graves.

Pound, E., 'Translators of Greek: Early Translators of Homer', in T. S. Eliot (ed.), *Literary Essays of Ezra Pound* (London, 1960).

Webb, E. T., (ed.), *English Romantic Hellenism 1700–1824* (Manchester, 1982).

Index

Addison, Joseph, 38, 52
Aeschylus, 18
Ainsworth, Harrison, 46
Apollonius Rhodius, 4
Arnold, Matthew, 13, 27, 42, 45, 47, 54
Auerbach, Erich, 10–11, 65

Bassnett, Susan, 66
Bentley, Richard, 32–3, 57
Bible, 36–7, 55
    Authorized Version, 18, 47, 54, 55, 56
Blake, William, 61
Boccaccio, Giovanni, 18
Bradbrook, M. C., 27
Broome, William, 34
Browne, Sir Thomas, 8
Buchan, John, 49
Bunting, Basil, 62
Butcher, S. H., 46, 68
Butler, Samuel, 8, 47–8, 49

Carne-Ross, Donald, 56
Chapman, George, 1–2, 16–28, 34, 35, 36, 37, 40, 42, 43, 45, 49, 54, 56, 57, 61
Chatterton, Thomas, 12
Chaucer, Geoffrey, 18
Clarke, Charles Cowden, 16
Cohen, J. M., 2
Coleridge, Samuel Taylor, 26–7, 41–2
Congreve, William, 31

Cowper, William, 41, 55

Dacier, Anne, 32, 35, 36, 45, 52
Dante, 1
Dares Phrygius, 18
Derby, Lord, 56
Derrida, Jacques, 5, 6, 62
Dictys Cretensis, 18
Divus, Andreas, 20
Donne, John, 27
Dostoevsky, Fyodor, 2
Dryden, John, 28, 31, 32, 36, 40

Eliot, T. S., 1, 27, 28
Euripides, 18
Eustathius, 36

Fagles, Robert, 6, 56, 57, 59, 60, 64
Fenton, Elijah, 34
Ficino, Marsilio, 18, 20
Fielding, Henry, 46
Fitzgerald, Robert, 56, 57, 59, 60, 64

Guido (painter), 36

Hall, Arthur, 18–9, 20, 22, 24
Hobbes, Thomas, 31

Johnson, Samuel, 26, 33, 35, 41, 42
Jonson, Ben, 22
Joyce, James, 46, 64

Kavanagh, Patrick, 43–4
Keats, John, 16–7, 26, 42, 43
Keyes, Sidney, 29–30
Kneller, Sir Godfrey (painter), 36
Knox, Bernard, 56, 67–8

Lang, Andrew, 46–7, 48, 52, 54,
   56, 68
Lattimore, Richmond, 56, 57, 58–
   9, 60, 64
Lawrence, T. E., 48–9
Leaf, W., 46, 56
Lefevre, André, 66
Levi, Peter, 6
Logue, Christopher, 2, 6, 56–7,
   60–68
Longinus, 11
Lydgate, John, 18

Meredith, George, 48
Milton, John, 31, 36, 40
Motte, Antoine de la, 32
Murray, A. T., 56
Myers, E., 46, 56

Nabokov, Vladimir, 3
North, Sir Thomas, 18

Ogilby, John, 31
Orwell, George, 52
Ovid, 2, 17

Parry, Adam, 54–5
Parry, Millman, 9, 54, 58
Perrault, Charles, 31–2, 33
Plato, 18, 20
Plutarch, 18
Pope, Alexander, 2, 29–42, 44, 45,
   49, 51, 52, 55, 56, 57
Pound, Ezra, 4, 5, 14, 47, 61, 62,
   63

Proust, Marcel, 2

Radice, Betty, 50, 52, 68
Raphael (painter), 36
Richards, I. A., 4
Rieu, D. C. H., 50
Rieu, E. V., 2, 43–55, 56, 57, 58,
   61, 68
Romano, Julio (painter), 36
Rosa, Salvator (painter), 36
Rubens (painter), 36

Salel, Hugues, 19
Scapula, Joannes, 20
Schliemann, Heinrich
   (archaeologist), 9–10
Scott, Sir Walter, 46
Seneca, 18
Shakespeare, William, 18, 27
Sheppard, Samuel, 26
Shewring, Walter, 55, 60
Silk, Michael, 13, 59, 64
Sophocles, 18
Southey, Robert, 42
Spagnoletto (painter), 36
Spence, Joseph, 34
Sponde, Jean de (Spondanus),
   20, 35
Spenser, Edmund, 12, 27
Steiner, George, 5, 6, 44, 64, 67
Swinburne, A. C., 27, 28, 54

Trollope, Anthony, 54

Villon, François, 62
Virgil, 1, 2, 17, 30, 31, 32, 36, 51–
   2

Walcott, Derek, 64

Xenophanes, 11

Recent and
Forthcoming Titles
in the
New Series of

WRITERS AND
THEIR WORK

WRITERS AND THEIR WORK

RECENT & FORTHCOMING TITLES

Title	Author
Peter Ackroyd	*Susana Onega*
Kingsley Amis	*Richard Bradford*
W.H. Auden	*Stan Smith*
Aphra Behn	*Sue Wiseman*
Edward Bond	*Michael Mangan*
Emily Brontë	*Stevie Davies*
A.S. Byatt	*Richard Todd*
Angela Carter	*Lorna Sage*
Geoffrey Chaucer	*Steve Ellis*
Children's Literature	*Kimberley Reynolds*
Caryl Churchill	*Elaine Aston*
John Clare	*John Lucas*
S.T. Coleridge	*Stephen Bygrave*
Joseph Conrad	*Cedric Watts*
Crime Fiction	*Martin Priestman*
John Donne	*Stevie Davis*
George Eliot	*Josephine McDonagh*
English Translators of Homer	*Simeon Underwood*
Henry Fielding	*Jenny Uglow*
Elizabeth Gaskell	*Kate Flint*
William Golding	*Kevin McCarron*
Graham Greene	*Peter Mudford*
Hamlet	*Ann Thompson & Neil Taylor*
Thomas Hardy	*Peter Widdowson*
David Hare	*Jeremy Ridgman*
Tony Harrison	*Joe Kelleher*
William Hazlitt	*J. B. Priestley; R. L. Brett (intro. by Michael Foot)*
Seamus Heaney	*Andrew Murphy*
George Herbert	*T.S. Eliot (intro. by Peter Porter)*
Henry James – The Later Writing	*Barbara Hardy*
James Joyce	*Steven Connor*
Franz Kafka	*Michael Wood*
King Lear	*Terence Hawkes*
Philip Larkin	*Lawrence Lerner*
D.H. Lawrence	*Linda Ruth Williams*
Doris Lessing	*Elizabeth Maslen*
David Lodge	*Bernard Bergonzi*
Christopher Marlowe	*Thomas Healy*
Andrew Marvell	*Annabel Patterson*
Ian McEwan	*Kiernan Ryan*
A Midsummer Night's Dream	*Helen Hackett*
Walter Pater	*Laurel Brake*
Brian Patten	*Linda Cookson*
Sylvia Plath	*Elisabeth Bronfen*
Jean Rhys	*Helen Carr*
Richard II	*Margaret Healy*
Dorothy Richardson	*Carol Watts*
Romeo and Juliet	*Sasha Roberts*
Salman Rushdie	*Damien Grant*
Paul Scott	*Jacqueline Banerjee*
The Sensation Novel	*Lyn Pykett*
Edmund Spenser	*Colin Burrow*
J.R.R. Tolkien	*Charles Moseley*
Leo Tolstoy	*John Bayley*
Angus Wilson	*Peter Conradi*
Virginia Woolf	*Laura Marcus*
Working Class Fiction	*Ian Haywood*
W.B. Yeats	*Edward Larrissy*
Charlotte Yonge	*Alethea Hayter*

TITLES IN PREPARATION

Title	Author
Antony and Cleopatra	*Ken Parker*
Jane Austen	*Meenakshi Mukherjee*
Alan Ayckbourn	*Michael Holt*
J.G. Ballard	*Michel Delville*
Samuel Beckett	*Keir Elam*
William Blake	*John Beer*
Elizabeth Bowen	*Maud Ellmann*
Charlotte Brontë	*Sally Shuttleworth*
Caroline Dramatists	*Julie Sanders*
Daniel Defoe	*Jim Rigney*
Charles Dickens	*Rod Mengham*
Carol Ann Duffy	*Deryn Rees Jones*
E.M. Forster	*Nicholas Royle*
Brian Friel	*Geraldine Higgins*
The *Gawain* Poetry	*John Burrow*
Gothic Literature	*Emma Clery*
Henry IV	*Peter Bogdanov*
Henrik Ibsen	*Sally Ledger*
Geoffrey Hill	*Andrew Roberts*
Kazuo Ishiguro	*Cynthia Wong*
Ben Jonson	*Anthony Johnson*
Julius Caesar	*Mary Hamer*
John Keats	*Kelvin Everest*
Rudyard Kipling	*Jan Montefiore*
Charles and Mary Lamb	*Michael Baron*
Langland: *Piers Plowman*	*Claire Marshall*
C.S. Lewis	*William Gray*
Katherine Mansfield	*Helen Haywood*
Measure for Measure	*Kate Chedgzoy*
Vladimir Nabokov	*Neil Cornwell*
Old English Verse	*Graham Holderness*
Alexander Pope	*Pat Rogers*
Dennis Potter	*Derek Paget*
Lord Rochester	*Germaine Greer*
Christina Rossetti	*Kathryn Burlinson*
Mary Shelley	*Catherine Sharrock*
P.B. Shelley	*Paul Hamilton*
Stevie Smith	*Alison Light*
Wole Soyinka	*Mpalive Msiska*
Laurence Sterne	*Manfred Pfister*
Tom Stoppard	*Nicholas Cadden*
The Tempest	*Gordon McMullan*
Charles Tomlinson	*Tim Clark*
Anthony Trollope	*Andrew Sanders*
Derek Walcott	*Stewart Brown*
John Webster	*Thomas Sorge*
Mary Wollstonecraft	*Jane Moore*
Women Romantic Poets	*Anne Janowitz*
Women Writers of the 17th Century	*Ramona Wray*
William Wordsworth	*Nicholas Roe*